Math Contests
Grades 7 and 8
(and Algebra Course 1)
Volume 5

School Years
2001-2002 through 2005-2006

Written by

Steven R. Conrad • Daniel Flegler

Published by MATH LEAGUE PRESS
Printed in the United States of America

Cover art by Bob DeRosa

Phil Frank Cartoons Copyright © 1993 by CMS

First Printing, 2006

Copyright © 2006
by Mathematics Leagues Inc.
All Rights Reserved

Math League Press
P.O. Box 17
Tenafly, NJ 07670-0017

ISBN 0-940805-16-2

Preface

Math Contests—Grades 7 and 8, Volume 5 is the fifth volume in our series of problem books for grades 7 and 8. The first four volumes contain the contests given in the school years 1979-1980 through 2000-2001. This volume contains the contests given from 2001-2002 through 2005-2006. (You can use the order form on page 154 to order any of our 15 books.)

This book is divided into three sections for ease of use by students and teachers. You'll find the contests in the first section. Each contest consists of 30 or 40 multiple-choice questions that you can do in 30 minutes. On each 3-page contest, the questions on the 1st page are generally straightforward, those on the 2nd page are moderate in difficulty, and those on the 3rd page are more difficult. In the second section of the book, you'll find detailed solutions to all the contest questions. In the third and final section of the book are the letter answers to each contest. In this section, you'll also find rating scales you can use to rate your performance.

Many people prefer to consult the answer section rather than the solution section when first reviewing a contest. We believe that reworking a problem when you know the answer (but *not* the solution) often leads to increased understanding of problem-solving techniques.

Each school year, we sponsor an Annual 7th Grade Mathematics Contest, an Annual 8th Grade Mathematics Contest, and an Annual Algebra Course 1 Mathematics Contest. A student may participate in the contest on grade level or for any higher grade level. For example, students in grade 7 (or below) may participate in the 8th Grade Contest. *Any* student may participate in the Algebra Course 1 Contest. Starting with the 1991-92 school year, students have been permitted to use calculators on any of our contests.

Steven R. Conrad & Daniel Flegler, contest authors

Acknowledgments

For demonstrating the meaning of selflessness on a daily basis, special thanks to Grace Flegler.

To Mark Motyka, we offer our gratitude for his assistance over the years.

To Jeannine Kolbush, who did an awesome proofreading job, thanks!

ii

Table Of Contents

The Contests

● ●

2001-2002 through 2005-2006

7th Grade Contests

2001-2002 through 2005-2006

2001-2002 Annual 7th Grade Contest

Tuesday, February 19 or 26, 2002

7

Instructions

- **Time** You will have only *30 minutes* working time for this contest. You might be *unable* to finish all 40 questions in the time allowed.

- **Scores** Please remember that *this is a contest, not a test*—and there is no "passing" or "failing" score. Few students score as high as 30 points (75% correct). Students with half that, 15 points, *should be commended!*

- **Format and Point Value** This is a multiple-choice contest. Each answer is an A, B, C, or D. Write each answer in the *Answers* column to the right of each question. A correct answer is worth 1 point. Unanswered questions get no credit. You **may** use a calculator.

1. $50 + 100 + 150 + 200 = 4 \times$ _?_ A) 75 B) 100 C) 125 D) 133	1.
2. I began with $6.80 in dimes. I made 10 piles of dimes, each with the same number of dimes. Of the following, which could have been the number of dimes left over? A) 12 B) 24 C) 36 D) 48	2.
3. Round the sum $(0.999 + 8.88)$ to the nearest hundredth. A) 1.89 B) 9.879 C) 9.88 D) 18.87	3.
4. If I finished my 17-hour race against the clock at midnight, I began at A) 5 A.M. B) 7 A.M. C) 5 P.M. D) 7 P.M.	4.
5. $4^2 + 2^2 = 5^2 -$ _?_ A) 1 B) 2 C) 4 D) 5	5.
6. Of the following, which has the greatest value? A) 10^{10} B) 10×100 C) 10×10 D) 10×1^{10}	6.
7. $3^3 + 3^2 + 3^1 =$ A) 3×5 B) 3×6 C) 3×11 D) 3×13	7.
8. Folding a square in half along one of its diagonals forms two A) triangles B) rhombuses C) squares D) rectangles	8.
9. $\frac{1}{2} \times 1$ day $=$ _?_ $\times 1$ week A) $\frac{1}{7}$ B) $\frac{2}{7}$ C) $\frac{1}{14}$ D) $\frac{1}{28}$	9.
10. Ten million divided by 100 thousand equals A) 10 B) 100 C) 1000 D) 10 000	10.
11. A ream of paper contains 500 sheets. A case of 20 reams contains A) 25 sheets B) 500 sheets C) 1000 sheets D) 10 000 sheets	11.
12. Of the following, which has the greatest hundredths' digit? A) 79.68 B) 86.79 C) 97.86 D) 678.9	12.
13. When I multiply 111 by 999, the product will contain _?_ digits. A) 6 B) 5 C) 4 D) 3	13.
14. The number 40 is 30 more than 40 less than A) 70 B) 50 C) 30 D) 10	14.
15. I read 3 science fiction books, 4 math books, and 1 cookbook. What percent of these books were non-fiction? A) 37.5% B) 50% C) 60% D) 62.5%	15.

Go on to the next page ▮▶ **7**

16. If the square root of the perimeter of a square is 6, then the area of this square is
    A) 36   B) 64   C) 81   D) 144

16.

17. I sell "HELP" flags in only the following ways: 3 for $1, 2 for 75¢, and/or 1 for 40¢. The *least* for which I sell 35 HELP flags is
    A) $11.75   B) $11.90
    C) $12.00   D) $14.00

17.

18. $(2 \times 500) + (2 \times 501) =$
    A) $2 + (500 \times 501)$ B) $2 \times (500 + 501)$
    C) $(2 + 2) \times (500 + 501)$ D) $(2 \times 2) + (500 \times 501)$

18.

19. Which is the reciprocal of $\frac{8}{3} \times \frac{13}{18}$?
    A) $\frac{3}{8} \times \frac{13}{18}$ B) $\frac{3}{13} \times \frac{8}{18}$ C) $\frac{8}{3} \times \frac{18}{13}$ D) $\frac{3}{8} \times \frac{18}{13}$

19.

20. I'm equilateral. My perimeter is 36. My side is longest when I'm
    A) a triangle   B) a square   C) a rhombus   D) a hexagon

20.

21. How many whole-number factors of 36 are divisible by 2?
    A) 5   B) 6   C) 7   D) 8

21.

22. Increasing the average of 20 numbers by 2 increases their sum by
    A) 2   B) 10   C) 22   D) 40

22.

23. $\frac{2+3+4}{8+9+10} = \frac{?}{(8-1)+(9-1)+(10-1)}$
    A) 4   B) 6   C) 8   D) 9

23.

24. If 5 scoops of ice cream weigh 2 kg, then 13 scoops weigh
    A) $\frac{13}{10}$ kg   B) 5 kg   C) $\frac{26}{5}$ kg   D) 7 kg

24.

25. Of the following, $\sqrt{4} + \sqrt{16}$ is closest in value to
    A) $\sqrt{12}$ B) $\sqrt{20}$ C) $\sqrt{64}$ D) $\sqrt{100}$

25.

26. $\frac{1}{4}$ of $\frac{1}{4}\% =$ A) $\frac{1}{16}\%$ B) $\frac{1}{8}\%$ C) $\frac{1}{4}\%$ D) 1%

26.

27. How long is a diameter of a circle whose area is π cm^2?
    A) π cm   B) 2π cm   C) 1 cm   D) 2 cm

27.

28. What is the greatest common factor of $\sqrt{16}$ and $\sqrt{64}$?
    A) 16   B) 8   C) 4   D) 2

28.

29. Divide a square of side-length 6 into four triangles by drawing both diagonals of the square. The area of one of the triangles is
    A) 6   B) 9   C) $9\sqrt{2}$ D) 18

29.

Go on to the next page ⫸ **7**

30. How many prime numbers less than 200 are 1 more than the square of an integer?

    A) 5   B) 6   C) 9   D) 14

    30.

31. Pat's current age will triple in 18 years. Twice Pat's current age is

    A) 9 years   B) 12 years   C) 18 years   D) 24 years

    31.

32. The median of $\frac{1}{6}, \frac{1}{3}, \frac{1}{2}, \frac{1}{4}, \frac{1}{5}, \frac{1}{7}$ is

    A) $\frac{1}{9}$ B) $\frac{1}{4.5}$ C) $\frac{1}{3}$ D) $\frac{9}{40}$

    32.

33. In a poll of more than 1 million people, exactly $16\frac{2}{3}\%$ felt run-down. The exact number of people polled could have been _?_ million.

    A) 2   B) 4   C) 6   D) 8

    33.

34. What fraction of a meter is $\frac{35}{4}$ cm?

    A) $\frac{1}{25}$ B) $\frac{7}{80}$ C) $\frac{4}{35}$ D) $\frac{35}{4}$

    34.

35. $\sqrt{81} = (\underline{\ ?\ })^2$

    A) $\sqrt{3}$ B) 3   C) $3\sqrt{3}$ D) 9

    35.

36. The least possible sum of a positive number and its reciprocal is

    A) 2.5   B) 2   C) 1   D) 0

    36.

37. If the lengths of 3 sides of a triangle are consecutive integers, which of the following could be the perimeter of the triangle?

    A) 2000   B) 2001   C) 2002   D) 2003

    37.

38. $\left(\frac{1}{2} \times \frac{1}{3}\right) \div (2 \times 3) = \underline{\ ?\ } \times \frac{1}{3}$

    A) $\frac{1}{12}$ B) $\frac{1}{72}$ C) 3   D) 36

    38.

39. I drive at a speed of 40 km/hr. I can drive 50% farther in 50% less time if I increase my speed to

    A) 60 km/hr   B) 80 km/hr
    C) 120 km/hr   D) 160 km/hr

    39.

40. How many positive even numbers are factors of $3^5 \times 2^5$?

    A) 5   B) 6   C) 25   D) 30

    40.

The end of the contest 👉 **7**

Visit our Web site at http://www.mathleague.com

Solutions on Page 73 • Answers on Page 138

2002-2003 Annual 7th Grade Contest

Tuesday, February 18 or 25, 2003

7

Instructions

- **Time** You will have only *30 minutes* working time for this contest. You might be *unable* to finish all 40 questions in the time allowed.

- **Scores** Please remember that *this is a contest, not a test*—and there is no "passing" or "failing" score. Few students score as high as 30 points (75% correct). Students with half that, 15 points, *should be commended!*

- **Format and Point Value** This is a multiple-choice contest. Each answer is an A, B, C, or D. Write each answer in the *Answers* column to the right of each question. A correct answer is worth 1 point. Unanswered questions get no credit. You **may** use a calculator.

	Answers
1. The sum $44\,444 + 88\,888$ equals the product $66\,666 \times$ _?_ . A) 2 B) 6 C) 20 D) $66\,666$	1.
2. The tens' digit of 642 is the double of A) 1 B) 2 C) 3 D) 4	2.
3. Which sum represents a prime number? A) 243+40 B) 497+28 C) 640+42 D) 720+81	3.
4. $202+2002 = 203+2003 -$ _?_ A) 1 B) 2 C) 3 D) 4	4.
5. In the world of dog figure skating, if 2 hips = 1 hop, and 2 hops = 4 hip-hops, then 8 hip-hops = _?_ hips. A) 2 B) 4 C) 8 D) 16 	5.
6. $(2+4+6)^2 =$ A) $(1+2+3)^4$ B) $(1+2+3)\times 2$ C) $(1+2+3)^2\times 4$ D) $2^2+4^2+6^2$	6.
7. Round 99.99 to the nearest hundredth. A) 100.09 B) 100 C) 99.99 D) 99.1	7.
8. $(200\times 300) + (20\times 30) + (2\times 3) = (2\times 3)\times$ _?_ A) 111 B) $10\,101$ C) $60\,600$ D) $60\,606$	8.
9. Each of the following sums is a factor of $33+66+99$ _except_ A) 1+2+3 B) 3+6+9 C) 3+3+3 D) 9+9+9	9.
10. The additive inverse of $\frac{1}{3}$ is A) $-\frac{1}{3}$ B) -3 C) $\frac{2}{3}$ D) 3	10.
11. What is the perimeter of the top of a square pizza box that just manages to hold a circular pizza whose radius is 70 cm? A) 140 cm B) 140π cm C) 280 cm D) 560 cm	11.
12. $\frac{10}{8}\times\frac{8}{6}\times\frac{6}{4}\times\frac{4}{2} = \frac{8}{10}\times\frac{6}{8}\times\frac{4}{6}\times\frac{2}{4}\times$ _?_ A) 1 B) 4 C) 16 D) 25	12.
13. The average number of grams per burger in a Burger Bash burger is numerically equal to the average number of days per year during the past four years. That number is nearest to A) 365.00 B) 365.25 C) 365.33 D) 365.50 	13.
14. $5\times$ _?_ $= 5 \div \frac{2}{6}$. A) 4 B) 3 C) $\frac{3}{2}$ D) $\frac{1}{3}$	14.

Go on to the next page ▮▮▮➡ 7

15. Of the following numbers, which has the greatest tenths' digit?

   A) 0.3073   B) 3.073   C) 30.73   D) 307.3

15.

16. If a diagonal of one square is a side of a second square, then the region in which these two squares overlap is a

   A) triangle   B) square   C) rhombus   D) rectangle

16.

17. What percent of the total value of 50 quarters is 50 dimes?

   A) 10%   B) 30%   C) 35%   D) 40%

17.

18. $(999 \times 1000) - (999 \times 998) =$

   A) $1000+999$ B) $1000+998$ C) $1000-998$ D) $1000-999$

18.

19. My friends and I each volunteered at a charity car wash from noon until 30 minutes before midnight. We each washed cars for _?_ minutes.

   A) 330   B) 690   C) 1020   D) 1140

19.

20. $77^2 \times (77 \times 77)^2 =$

   A) 77^5 B) $77^2 \times 77^3$ C) $77^2 \times 77^4$ D) 3×77^2

20.

21. $3 \div 5 \div 7 =$ A) $\frac{3}{35}$ B) $\frac{7}{21}$ C) $\frac{15}{7}$ D) $\frac{21}{5}$

21.

22. $\left(1-\frac{1}{4}\right)+\left(1-\frac{1}{2}\right)+\left(1-\frac{1}{4}\right) =$ A) $\frac{3}{4}$ B) 1 C) $\frac{3}{2}$ D) 2

22.

23. The reciprocal of the quotient $\left(3 \div \frac{1}{6}\right)$ is

   A) $\frac{1}{3} \times \frac{1}{6}$ B) $\frac{1}{3} \times 6$ C) $3 \times \frac{1}{6}$ D) 3×6

23.

24. What is the largest multiple of 2 that is a factor of 72?

   A) 2   B) 8   C) 36   D) 72

24.

25. If I have $10 in nickels and you have $7 in dimes, then I have _?_ more coins than you.

   A) 30   B) 70   C) 130   D) 140

25.

26. The product of my 3 integers is odd. Their sum must be

   A) odd   B) even   C) positive   D) negative

26.

27. $\sqrt{64} - \sqrt{9} =$ A) $\sqrt{55}$ B) $\sqrt{45}$ C) $\sqrt{25}$ D) $\sqrt{5}$

27.

28. If 345 ♣ 54 = 334 ♣ 43, then ♣ could represent

   A) +   B) −   C) ×   D) ÷

28.

Go on to the next page ⏵ **7**

11

29. $\frac{4}{10}$ of 40 = _?_% of 4   A) 16   B) 40   C) 160   D) 400 | 29.

30. What is the tens' digit of the largest odd factor of 100 000 000? | 30.
     A) 0   B) 2   C) 4   D) 6

31. The sum of 9 consecutive integers is *not* always divisible by | 31.
     A) 1   B) 3   C) 6   D) 9

32. How many tiles will Rent-A-Kid need to install a | 32.
     single row of square tiles, each with side-length 1,
     along all 4 edges of the floor in a 12 × 16 room?
     A) 52   B) 56   C) 58   D) 60

33. 0.4^2 is less than   A) 0.2^2 B) 0.2^3 C) 0.4 D) 0.4^4 | 33.

34. A triangle with perimeter 8 and integer side-lengths must be | 34.
     A) isosceles   B) right   C) obtuse   D) equilateral

35. If $(1/10)^{100}$ = 0.00 . . . 1, then the total number of times that a | 35.
     0 appears to the right of the decimal point and left of the 1 is
     A) 98   B) 99   C) 100   D) 101

36. Lance sells 60 bikes each month. If 1/3 of the racing bikes he | 36.
     sells each month equals 1/12 of all the bikes he sells each
     month, how many racing bikes does Lance sell each month?
     A) 20   B) 15   C) 12   D) 5

37. A square and a circle can have at most _?_ points in common. | 37.
     A) 2   B) 4   C) 6   D) 8

38. I plan to give a *total* of 3 (identical) | 38.
     slices of pizza to Ali, Bob, and Carl.
     Each person will get 0, 1, 2, or 3 slices.
     In how many different ways can I dis-
     tribute these 3 slices of pizza?
     A) 8   B) 9   C) 10   D) 12

39. A *perfect square* is the square of an integer. Of the integers from 2 | 39.
     through 99, how many have at least one *perfect square* factor > 1?
     A) 36   B) 38   C) 40   D) 44

40. The three hands of an accurate 12-hour clock make a total of | 40.
     _?_ complete revolutions around the clock's face every 24 hours.
     A) 72   B) 733   C) 1466   D) 10 104

The end of the contest ✍ **7**

Visit our Web site at http://www.mathleague.com

2003-04 Annual 7th Grade Contest

Tuesday, February 17 or 24, 2004

Instructions

7

- **Time** You will have only *30 minutes* working time for this contest. You might be *unable* to finish all 40 questions in the time allowed.

- **Scores** Please remember that *this is a contest, not a test*—and there is no "passing" or "failing" score. Few students score as high as 30 points (75% correct). Students with half that, 15 points, *should be commended!*

- **Format and Point Value** This is a multiple-choice contest. Each answer is an A, B, C, or D. Write each answer in the *Answers* column to the right of each question. A correct answer is worth 1 point. Unanswered questions get no credit. You **may** use a calculator.

1. $(10 + 10) \times (10 - 10) =$ A) 0 B) 20 C) 190 D) 990	1.	
2. What is the remainder when $1900 + 190 + 19$ is divided by 5? A) 1 B) 2 C) 3 D) 4	2.	
3. $2 + (2 \times 2) + 2$ has the same value as A) $(2 + 2)^2$ B) $(2 \times 2)^2$ C) $2^2 \times 2^2$ D) $2^2 + 2^2$	3.	
4. Of the following, which is closest in value to 0.9? A) 0.8 B) 0.85 C) 0.89 D) 0.99	4.	
5. 30 minutes before 5 P.M. = 15 minutes after _?_ P.M. A) 5:15 B) 4:45 C) 4:30 D) 4:15	5.	
6. As my family watched, I won 50% of my horseshoe tosses. If I lost 18 times, then I won _?_ times. A) 36 B) 27 C) 18 D) 9	6.	
7. 1 km + 10 m + 100 cm = A) 111 m B) 1010 m C) 1011 m D) 1110 m	7.	
8. $4 + \frac{3}{2} = \frac{1}{2} + $ _?_ A) $4\frac{1}{2}$ B) 5 C) $5\frac{1}{2}$ D) 6	8.	
9. How many positive multiples of 4 are less than 100? A) 22 B) 24 C) 25 D) 26	9.	
10. Increasing each of 64 numbers by 2 increases their sum by A) 2 B) 32 C) 64 D) 128	10.	
11. Multiplying a number by 0.25 is the same as dividing it by A) 4 B) 400 C) 2.5 D) 25	11.	
12. 2000 − (the average of 1000 and 2000) = A) 50 B) 500 C) 1000 D) 1500	12.	
13. What is the volume of a rectangular solid with length 3, width 4, and height 2? A) 99 B) 24 C) 18 D) 9	13.	
14. Of 20 fund-raising volunteers, 4 supervise and 16 wash cars. What percent of the 20 volunteers are supervisors? A) 20% B) 25% C) 75% D) 80%	14.	

Go on to the next page ▐▶ **7**

14

15. 36 seconds is _?_ of 1 hour.   A) $\frac{1}{100}$ B) $\frac{36}{60}$ C) $\frac{1}{36}$ D) $\frac{1}{3600}$

15.

16. $(183 \times 999) - (182 \times 999) =$ A) 1   B) 182   C) 183   D) 999

16.

17. If my sister has 3 brothers and 2 sisters, then my brother has _?_ brothers and _?_ sisters.

   A) 2, 2   B) 2, 3   C) 3, 2   D) 3, 3

17.

18. $2\frac{1}{4} \times 2\frac{1}{4} \times 2\frac{1}{4} =$ A) $\frac{8}{64}$ B) $\frac{27}{64}$ C) $8\frac{1}{64}$ D) $\frac{729}{64}$

18.

19. As I waited for my ship to dock, I put nine Ping-Pong balls numbered 1 to 9 into an empty bag, then selected one ball at random. What was the probability that the number on the ball that I selected was even?

   A) $\frac{1}{5}$ B) $\frac{1}{4}$ C) $\frac{4}{9}$ D) $\frac{5}{9}$

19.

20. $\frac{1}{2} + \frac{1}{3} = 1 \div$ _?_   A) 6   B) $\frac{6}{5}$ C) $\frac{5}{6}$ D) $\frac{1}{5}$

20.

21. The reciprocal of any number greater than 1 is

   A) less than 1   B) more than 1   C) odd   D) negative

21.

22. 100 tenths = _?_ hundredths

   A) 10   B) 100   C) 1000   D) 10 000

22.

23. When the *Bike Teens* perform at the circus, for every performer that frowns, there are four that smile. This means that _?_ of the 80 *Bike Teens* smile while performing.

   A) 16   B) 20   C) 60   D) 64

23.

24. 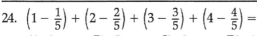 $\left(1 - \frac{1}{5}\right) + \left(2 - \frac{2}{5}\right) + \left(3 - \frac{3}{5}\right) + \left(4 - \frac{4}{5}\right) =$

   A) 0   B) 5   C) 8   D) 10

24.

25. In $\triangle ABC$, if $m \angle A = 80°$, then $m \angle C$ *cannot* be

   A) 80°   B) 90°   C) 95°   D) 105°

25.

26. $\sqrt{4^2} + \sqrt{12^2} = \sqrt{7^2} + \sqrt{?}$ A) 15^2 B) 9^2 C) 6^2 D) 3^2

26.

27. If the product of two positive primes is 87, then their sum is

   A) 20   B) 30   C) 32   D) 42

27.

28. 1% = 10 × _?_   A) 0.001   B) 0.01   C) 0.1   D) 1

28.

Go on to the next page ⏭ **7**

29. $3 \times \sqrt{25} = 5 \times \underline{?}$ A) $\sqrt{3}$ B) $\sqrt{9}$ C) $\sqrt{15}$ D) $\sqrt{81}$	29.
30. When you divide my fraction by yours, the result is 40. When you divide your fraction by mine, the result is A) 0.025 B) 0.25 C) 0.40 D) 2.50	30.
31. The area of rectangle R is 48. If its sides are whole numbers, then its perimeter *cannot* be A) 28 B) 38 C) 58 D) 98	31.
32. I have twice as many nickels as dimes. My dimes are worth \$3.30. My nickels are worth A) \$1.15 B) \$3.30 C) \$6.60 D) \$13.20	32.
33. Which is true? A) $\frac{3}{7} < \frac{4}{9}$ B) $\frac{6}{13} < \frac{4}{9}$ C) $\frac{8}{17} < \frac{4}{9}$ D) $\frac{2}{3} < \frac{4}{9}$	33.
34. The square of an integer is a *perfect square*. What is the smallest perfect square that is a multiple of 2, of 4, of 6, and of 8? A) 64 B) 144 C) 576 D) 2304	34.
35. $4^9 \div 9^4 = 2^{18} \div \underline{?}$ A) 81^3 B) 18^3 C) 7^8 D) 3^8	35.
36. The greatest common factor of 10×20 and 20×30 is A) 10 B) 10×10 C) 10×20 D) $10 \times 20 \times 30$	36.
37. $\frac{9}{7} \times \frac{7}{5} \times \frac{5}{3} = \frac{3}{5} \times \frac{5}{7} \times \frac{7}{9} \times \underline{?}$ A) 27 B) 18 C) 9 D) 3	37.
38. My dog's frisbee is in the shape of a circle whose area is $\frac{1}{\pi}$. How long is a radius of this frisbee? A) $\frac{1}{\pi}$ B) $\frac{1}{2\pi}$ C) $\frac{1}{\pi^2}$ D) $\frac{1}{2\pi^2}$	38.
39. What is the ones' digit of 2003^{2004}? [Hint: Look for a pattern.] A) 9 B) 7 C) 3 D) 1	39.
40. The value of the 100-term sum $\frac{1}{2} + \frac{3}{2} + \frac{5}{2} + ... + \frac{195}{2} + \frac{197}{2} + \frac{199}{2}$ is A) 5000 B) 10 000 C) 15 000 D) 20 000	40.

The end of the contest 🖎 **7**

2004-2005 Annual 7th Grade Contest

February 15 or 22, 2005

7

Instructions

- **Time** You will have only *30 minutes* working time for this contest. You might be *unable* to finish all 40 questions in the time allowed.

- **Scores** Please remember that *this is a contest, not a test*—and there is no "passing" or "failing" score. Few students score as high as 30 points (75% correct). Students with half that, 15 points, *should be commended!*

- **Format and Point Value** This is a multiple-choice contest. Each answer is an A, B, C, or D. Write each answer in the *Answers* column to the right of each question. A correct answer is worth 1 point. Unanswered questions get no credit. You **may** use a calculator.

1. If 84 players split themselves into teams, how many more teams can they form by splitting into teams of 4 instead of teams of 6?
   A) 5 B) 6 C) 7 D) 14

   1.

2. $0 \times 1 + 1 \times 10 + 0 \times 0 + 1 =$
   A) 0 B) 1 C) 3 D) 11

   2.

3. The three angles of a triangle can measure 20°, 40°, and
   A) 60° B) 80° C) 90° D) 120°

   3.

4. To the nearest tenth, $3456 \times 0.001 =$
   A) 0.3 B) 3.4 C) 3.5 D) 34.6

   4.

5. If my bad hair day began 720 minutes before 7:20 P.M., then my bad hair day began at
   A) 1:20 A.M. B) 7:20 A.M.
   C) 12:00 P.M. D) 7:08 P.M.

   5.

6. $500 + 500 + 500 + 500 + 500 = 10 \times \underline{\ ?\ }$
   A) 25 B) 50 C) 250 D) 2000

   6.

7. Of the whole numbers 10, 11, . . . , 98, 99, how many are greater than the sum of their digits?
   A) 88 B) 89 C) 90 D) 99

   7.

8. $1^3 + 2^4 =$ A) $1^4 + 3^2$ B) $1^3 + 4^2$ C) $1^2 + 4^3$ D) $1^1 + 3^4$

   8.

9. 7 is prime, so May 7th is a *prime* day. In all, May has $\underline{\ ?\ }$ prime days.
   A) 10 B) 11 C) 12 D) 13

   9.

10. $\frac{2}{3} \times \frac{4}{5} \times \frac{6}{7} \times \frac{7}{6} \times \frac{5}{4} \times \frac{3}{2} =$ A) 1 B) 3 C) 6 D) 12

    10.

11. 500 nickels = $\underline{\ ?\ }$ quarters
    A) 100 B) 250 C) 500 D) 2500

    11.

12. If a square's side-lengths are integers, its perimeter could be
    A) 33 B) 44 C) 55 D) 66

    12.

13. If 3 of every 150 astronauts walk on the moon, then $\underline{\ ?\ }$ % of all astronauts walk on the moon.
    A) 2 B) 3 C) 5 D) 50

    13.

14. Of the following, which *doesn't* reduce to $\frac{3}{5}$?
    A) $\frac{9}{15}$ B) $\frac{21}{35}$ C) $\frac{24}{40}$ D) $\frac{33}{50}$

    14.

15. $\sqrt{100} = \sqrt{36} + \sqrt{?}$
    A) 2 B) 4 C) 16 D) 64

    15.

Go on to the next page ⫸ 7

18

16. _?_ can be made from 2 squares that share a common side.
A) An octagon B) A hexagon C) A rectangle D) A triangle

16.

17. By how much does the sum $19+28+37+46+55+64+73+82+91$ exceed the sum $18+27+36+45+54+63+72+81+90$?
A) 9   B) 10   C) 90   D) 100

17.

18. Uncle Bookworm eats two books a week; Aunt Bookworm eats one book every two months. In a year, Uncle eats _?_ more books than Aunt.
A) 20   B) 40   C) 80   D) 98

18.

19. What is the largest odd factor of 81?
A) 3   B) 9   C) 27   D) 81

19.

20. $\left(\frac{2}{3}\right)^3 =$ A) 2   B) $\frac{6}{9}$ C) $\frac{8}{3}$ D) $\frac{8}{27}$

20.

21. *At most* how many students can sit in a row of 25 chairs, if seated students must be separated by at least one empty chair?
A) 11   B) 12   C) 13   D) 24

21.

22. The smallest multiple of 10 that's greater than 9×9 is
A) $9 \times 9 + 10$ B) 9.1×9.1 C) 9×10 D) 10×10

22.

23. The difference between $\frac{5}{6}$ and its reciprocal is
A) $\frac{1}{5}$ B) $\frac{1}{6}$ C) $\frac{1}{30}$ D) $\frac{11}{30}$

23.

24. On my scooter, the rear wheel's diameter is 6 cm more than the front wheel's. The rear wheel's circumference is _?_ cm more than the front wheel's.
A) 3π B) 6π C) 9π D) 36π

24.

25. A regular polygon is always
A) square   B) equilateral   C) scalene   D) isosceles

25.

26. If I divide my age by 5, the remainder is 3. Your age is twice mine. If I divide your age by 5, the remainder will be
A) 1   B) 2   C) 3   D) 4

26.

27. In a rectangle with perimeter 30 cm and area 56 cm^2, the longer side's length is _?_ cm more than that of the shorter side.
A) 1   B) 5   C) 20   D) 26

27.

28. If the sum of two whole numbers is 24 more than their difference, then one of the numbers *must* be
A) 0   B) 6   C) 12   D) 48

28.

Go on to the next page ⫸ 7

19

29. The first 12 contestants won an average of $80. The next 20 won an average of $70. The 32 contestants won an average of
    A) $73.75   B) $74.75   C) $75.00   D) $75.75 | 29.

30. $4^3 \times 4^3 =$ A) 16^9 B) 16^6 C) 4^9 D) 4^6 | 30.

31. At most ? circles of radius 1 with non-overlapping interiors can fit inside a square with side-length 4.
    A) 1   B) 4   C) 5   D) 16 | 31.

32. $0.1\% = 1\% - $?
    A) 0.009%   B) 0.09%   C) 0.9%   D) 10% | 32.

33. Today is my birthday. My age today, in months, is 72 times my age 5 years ago, in years. My age today, in years, is
    A) 6   B) 7   C) 8   D) 12 | 33.

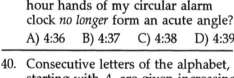

34. $\sqrt{\sqrt{81 \times 81 \times 81 \times 81}} =$
    A) 3   B) 9   C) 27   D) 81 | 34.

35. Of 2005 integers whose product is even, at most ? can be odd. | 35.
    A) 2005   B) 2004   C) 1   D) 0

36. The number ? equals one-fourth of its own reciprocal. | 36.
    A) $\frac{1}{2}$ B) $\frac{1}{4}$ C) 2   D) 4

37. How many of the numbers $11, 21, 31, 41, 51, 61, 71, 81, 91$ are prime? | 37.
    A) 4   B) 5   C) 6   D) 7

38. $(301 + 302 + 303 + \ldots + 325) - (1 + 2 + 3 + \ldots + 25) =$ | 38.
    A) 25   B) 2500   C) 5000   D) 7500

39. Of the following, which is the first time after 4:30 that the minute and hour hands of my circular alarm clock *no longer* form an acute angle? | 39.
    A) 4:36   B) 4:37   C) 4:38   D) 4:39

40. Consecutive letters of the alphabet, starting with A, are given increasing consecutive integer values. If $H+K+L+N = 2005$, then the average of all 26 of the consecutive integers is | 40.
    A) 491   B) 498   C) 503.5   D) 505.5

The end of the contest  **7**

Visit our Web site at http://www.mathleague.com

Solutions on Page 85 • Answers on Page 141

2005-2006 Annual 7th Grade Contest

February 21 or 28, 2006

Instructions

7

- **Time** You will have only *30 minutes* working time for this contest. You might be *unable* to finish all 40 questions in the time allowed.

- **Scores** Please remember that *this is a contest, not a test*—and there is no "passing" or "failing" score. Few students score as high as 30 points (75% correct). Students with half that, 15 points, *should be commended!*

- **Format and Point Value** This is a multiple-choice contest. Each answer is an A, B, C, or D. Write each answer in the *Answers* column to the right of each question. A correct answer is worth 1 point. Unanswered questions get no credit. You **may** use a calculator.

1. $24\,242 + 42\,424 = 22\,222 \times \underline{?\ }$
   A) 2   B) 3   C) 4   D) 6   1.

2. A pot of gold, just out of reach, weighs as many kg as the number of days it takes to go backwards from any Feb. 1 to the previous Mar. 1. That pot of gold weighs $\underline{?\ }$ kg.
   A) 335   B) 336   C) 337   D) 338   2.

3. Consecutive odd numbers differ by
   A) 0   B) 1   C) 2   D) 3   3.

4. $(18+19+20+21+22) \div 5 =$
   A) 19   B) 20   C) 20.5   D) 21   4.

5. $64 \div 8 \times 4 \times 2 =$
   A) 1   B) 4   C) 16   D) 64   5.

6. 10×500 cm $= 5 \times \underline{?\ }$ m
   A) 5000   B) 1000   C) 100   D) 10   6.

7. If twice my age in months is 120, then my age in years is
   A) 5   B) 10   C) 12   D) 60   7.

8. A square with even side-lengths *cannot* have a perimeter of
   A) 12   B) 16   C) 24   D) 32   8.

9. The sum $100+99+98$ exceeds the sum $99+98+97$ by
   A) 1   B) 3   C) 4   D) 97   9.

10. It takes $\underline{?\ }$ 8-slice pizzas to give 64 people 2 slices each.
   A) 32   B) 16   C) 8   D) 4   10.

11. $3^2 - 2^2 - 1^2 =$
   A) 0   B) 1   C) 3   D) 4   11.

12. If 1 Red River beaver eats as much as 6 White River beavers, and 3 White River beavers eat as much as 4 Green River beavers, then 5 Red River beavers eat as much as $\underline{?\ }$ Green River beavers.
   A) 20   B) 30   C) 40   D) 60   12.

13. Of the following, which has the greatest value?
   A) 1×10^2 B) 8×10^1 C) 10×8^1 D) 18×1^{10} 13.

14. 1 tenth $-$ 1 hundredth $=$
   A) 9.90   B) 0.99   C) 0.90   D) 0.09   14.

15. 6 halves $= \underline{?\ }$ thirds
   A) 3   B) 4   C) 9   D) 12   15.

Go on to the next page ▐▶ **7**

16. In the quotient $(20 \times 16 \times 12 \times 8) \div (5 \times 4 \times 3 \times 2)$, the remainder is

    A) 0　　　　B) 1　　　　C) 2　　　　D) 4

    16.

17. What is the largest odd factor of 6^4?

    A) 3　　　　B) 3^3　　　　C) 9^2　　　　D) 9^4

    17.

18. Two points that lie on a circle of radius 2 *cannot* be _?_ unit(s) apart.

    A) 1　　　　B) 2　　　　C) 4　　　　D) 4π

    18.

19. The quotient $\frac{1}{2} \div \frac{3}{4}$ equals the quotient $2 \div$ _?_ .

    A) $\frac{3}{4}$　　　　B) $\frac{4}{3}$　　　　C) 3　　　　D) 4

    19.

20. The number of nickels in $40 is 4 times the number of dimes in

    A) $10　　　　B) $20　　　　C) $80　　　　D) $160

    20.

21. Which number is $\frac{1}{5}$ of the reciprocal of $\left(\frac{1}{2} + \frac{1}{3}\right)$?

    A) $\frac{6}{25}$　　　　B) $\frac{6}{5}$　　　　C) $\frac{1}{6}$　　　　D) 1

    21.

22. If $\frac{1}{3}$ of my pockets are empty, and $\frac{1}{3}$ of those have a hole, what fraction of my pockets should *not* be classified as empty pockets with a hole?

    A) $\frac{1}{3}$　　B) $\frac{5}{9}$　　C) $\frac{2}{3}$　　D) $\frac{8}{9}$

    22.

23. 1% of 1 = 10% of _?_

    A) 10　　B) 1　　C) 0.10　　D) 0.01

    23.

24. What is the product of 15 consecutive integers whose average is 7?

    A) 0　　　　B) 7　　　　C) 105　　　　D) 5040

    24.

25. $\sqrt{36+64} = \sqrt{4} \times \sqrt{?}$

    A) 16　　　　B) 25　　　　C) 36　　　　D) 49

    25.

26. In a triangle whose sides all have integer lengths and whose perimeter is 24, the length of the longest side is *at most*

    A) 11　　　　B) 13　　　　C) 16　　　　D) 22

    26.

27. $21+42+63+84+105+126 = 21 \times$ _?_

    A) 6　　　　B) 7　　　　C) 21　　　　D) 42

    27.

28. If a dirt truck carries 20 loads every day, then what percent of a 350-load job does this truck carry in 7 days?

    A) 42%　　B) 40%　　C) 30%　　D) 6%

    28.

29. $\frac{1+2+3}{2+4+6} + \frac{4+8+12}{1+2+3} =$

    A) 2　　B) $\frac{8}{3}$　　C) 4　　D) $\frac{9}{2}$

    29.

23

Go on to the next page ⇒ **7**

30. Two different diameters of the same circle *cannot*
    A) be perpendicular   B) be parallel
    C) be equal in length   D) have a point in common

30.

31. $999^2 = \sqrt{999} \times \sqrt{?}$
    A) 999   B) 999^2 C) 999^3 D) 999^4

31.

32. At the seashore, when I put a large shell to my ear, I heard the largest 3-digit prime. In that prime, the only *digit* that's prime is
    A) 1   B) 3   C) 5   D) 7

32.

33. The tens' digit of the product $5^{2005} \times 2005^5$ is
    A) 0   B) 2   C) 4   D) 5

33.

34. Of the whole-number multiples of 36 that are both more than 36 and less than 36^2, how many are squares of whole numbers?
    A) 0   B) 4   C) 9   D) 16

34.

35. $\frac{5}{3} \div \frac{3}{5} = \frac{3}{5} \times \underline{\ ?\ }$
    A) $\frac{2}{5}$ B) $\frac{5}{3}$ C) $\frac{50}{18}$ D) $\frac{125}{27}$

35.

36. (the product of all the factors of 100) ÷ (100) =
    A) 1   B) 100   C) 100^4 D) 10^7

36.

37. If $a \triangle b \triangle c = a \times c + b \times c$, then $7 \triangle 8 \triangle 9 =$
    A) 128   B) 135   C) 272   D) 639

37.

38. $1 + \dfrac{2}{3 + \dfrac{4}{5}} =$
    A) $1\frac{10}{19}$ B) $1\frac{10}{12}$ C) $2\frac{3}{7}$ D) $8\frac{2}{5}$

38.

39. Speedy Rabbit ran once around an 800 m track in 5 minutes. If Speedy had increased his average speed by _?_, he would have finished in 20% less time.
    A) 20%   B) 25%   C) 30%   D) 40%

39.

40. Fifty rabbits began a 30-minute race. Whenever 2 dropped out, 1 joined in haste. If 2 dropped out 13 times, tell me then, how many rabbits were in the race at the end?
    A) 20   B) 24   C) 37   D) 39

40.

The end of the contest ✍ **7**

Visit our Web site at http://www.mathleague.com

Solutions on Page 89 • Answers on Page 142

8th Grade Contests

2001-2002 through 2005-2006

2001-2002 Annual 8th Grade Contest

Tuesday, February 19 or 26, 2002

Instructions

8

- **Time** You will have only *30 minutes* working time for this contest. You might be *unable* to finish all 40 questions in the time allowed.

- **Scores** Please remember that *this is a contest, not a test*—and there is no "passing" or "failing" score. Few students score as high as 30 points (75% correct). Students with half that, 15 points, *should be commended!*

- **Format and Point Value** This is a multiple-choice contest. Each answer is an A, B, C, or D. Write each answer in the *Answers* column to the right of each question. A correct answer is worth 1 point. Unanswered questions get no credit. You **may** use a calculator.

1. $201 + 401 + 601 = 101 + 301 + 501 + \underline{\ ?\ }$
   A) 100   B) 200   C) 300   D) 600

2. My father got upset when he saw my test grade. My grade was a product of two consecutive integers. My test grade could have been
   A) 45   B) 48   C) 54   D) 56

3. Of the following, which number is *greatest*?
   A) 0.011   B) 0.0111   C) 0.0101   D) 0.01

4. How many pennies equal one-tenth of ten dollars?
   A) 1   B) 10   C) 100   D) 1000

5. On the average, it rains 125 days each year in New York City. To the nearest 1%, it rains $\underline{\ ?\ }$% of the days in New York City.
   A) 34   B) 33   C) 13   D) 3

6. Each of the following is a factor of 444 444 444 *except*
   A) 4   B) 11   C) 111   D) 444

7. If 2003 is the largest of 3 consecutive integers, the smallest is
   A) 1999   B) 2000   C) 2001   D) 2005

8. $0.77 \times 111 = 77 \times 1.11 \times \underline{\ ?\ }$
   A) 0.01   B) 0.1   C) 1   D) 10

9. The reciprocal of a positive prime number is always
   A) odd   B) even   C) prime   D) positive

10. Which of the following is a whole number?
    A) $\frac{135}{7}$ B) $\frac{145}{9}$ C) $\frac{155}{11}$ D) $\frac{175}{7}$

11. What is the side-length of a square that has the same perimeter as an equilateral triangle with side-length 12?
    A) 3   B) 9   C) 16   D) 36

12. $1 + 2 \times 3 + 4 = 1 + 2 \times (3 + \underline{\ ?\ })$
    A) 2   B) 4   C) 5   D) 7

13. Gumballs cost 1¢ each, and gumdrops cost 2¢ each. How much more will it cost to buy 100 gumdrops than 50 gumballs?
    A) $1.00   B) $1.50   C) $2.00   D) $3.50

14. $\dfrac{7+8}{(7 \times 7) + (7 \times 8)} = \dfrac{1}{7} + \underline{\ ?\ }$
    A) 0   B) $\frac{1}{7}$ C) $\frac{1}{8}$ D) 1

15. $16 \times 25 \times 36 = (\underline{\ ?\ })^2$
    A) 15   B) 25   C) 77   D) 120

Answers column:
1.
2.
3.
4.
5.
6.
7.
8.
9.
10.
11.
12.
13.
14.
15.

Go on to the next page ⫸ **8**

16. What is the average measure of the angles in an acute triangle?

    A) 30°   B) 45°   C) 60°   D) 90°

16.

17. How many digits are in the product $99\,999 \times 99\,999$?

    A) 11   B) 10   C) 8   D) 5

17.

18. $9 \times 9 + 9 \div 9 - 9 =$

    A) 73   B) 45   C) 9   D) 1

18.

19. _?_ is twice as many days after Sunday as it is before Tuesday.

    A) Mon.   B) Wed.   C) Thurs.   D) Sat.

19.

20. 0.2% of 2% of 20 =

    A) 0.0008   B) 0.008   C) 0.08   D) 8.0

20.

21. If the product of two numbers is positive, their sum *cannot* be

    A) positive   B) negative   C) 0   D) a fraction

21.

22. What is the remainder when 3^9 is divided by 9^3?

    A) $3 - 3$ B) 3×3 C) $3 + 9$ D) 3×9

22.

23. The number 33 uses 2 non-zero digits. Altogether, the 50 whole numbers from 1 through 50 use _?_ *non-zero* digits.

    A) 90   B) 86   C) 50   D) 45

23.

24. If 3 out of 4 people are into hot soup, then _?_ out of 700 are into hot soup.

    A) 475   B) 500   C) 525   D) 550

24.

25. Reversing the digits of _?_ decreases its value by close to 50%.

    A) 2991   B) 3002   C) 4008   D) 6003

25.

26. Which of the following numbers is less than $\frac{1}{4}$?

    A) $\sqrt{\frac{1}{4}}$ B) $\frac{1}{4} \div \frac{1}{4}$ C) $\left(\frac{1}{4}\right)^2$ D) $1 \div \frac{1}{4}$

26.

27. If $a \,❖\, b = a \times b + b^2$, what is the value of $8 \,❖\, 6$?

    A) 100   B) 84   C) 54   D) 48

27.

28. The product of a positive number and its additive inverse is

    A) greater than 1   B) 1   C) 0   D) less than 0

28.

29. If one person stands at each vertex of a regular hexagon, what is the fewest number of people who must move so that all will be standing in a straight line?

    A) 5   B) 4   C) 3   D) 2

29.

Go on to the next page ⮕ **8**

30. How many of the first 1000 positive integers are multiples of all four of the numbers 2, 3, 4, and 5?

    A) 8   B) 9   C) 16   D) 17

    30.

31. If the sum of 2 integers is 20, their product could equal any of the following *except*

    A) –125   B) –21   C) 19   D) 60

    31.

32. What is the ratio of the number of seconds in 45 minutes to the number of seconds in one hour?

    A) 1:2   B) 1:4   C) 3:4   D) 4:3

    32.

33. _?_ of 50 = 50% + 50%

    A) 1%   B) 2%   C) 50%   D) 100%

    33.

34. The absolute value of the difference between a number and its reciprocal can be as small as _?_ , but no smaller.

    A) 0   B) $\frac{1}{5}$ C) $\frac{7}{12}$ D) $\frac{3}{2}$

    34.

35. If 40% of the number of people shipwrecked on my island equals 50% of the number shipwrecked on yours, then the number of people shipwrecked on my island is _?_ of the number shipwrecked on yours.

    A) 80%   B) 90%   C) 120%   D) 125%

    35.

36. On a math test, twelve 8th graders averaged 80.00, while twenty 7th graders averaged 70.00. For all 32 students, the average was

    A) 72.25   B) 73.75   C) 74.75   D) 75.00

    36.

37. $\left(\sqrt{\sqrt{x}}\right)^4 =$ A) $\sqrt{x}$ B) x C) x^2 D) x^4

    37.

38. In a rectangle with area 72 cm^2 and perimeter 34 cm, the length of the longer side exceeds that of the shorter side by

    A) 1 cm   B) 6 cm   C) 18 cm   D) 38 cm

    38.

39. Three small congruent circles, surrounded by a large circle, have their centers on a diameter of the large circle, as shown. If the area of the shaded region is 24π, what is the area of one small circle?

    A) 12π B) 9π C) 4π D) π

    39.

40. $\dfrac{1}{2^1} + \dfrac{1}{2^2} + \dfrac{1}{2^3} + \ldots + \dfrac{1}{2^{50}} = \dfrac{(2^{49} + 2^{48} + 2^{47} + \ldots + 2^1) + \underline{\ ?\ }}{2^{50}}$

    A) 0   B) 1   C) 2^{50} D) $1 + 2^{50}$

    40.

The end of the contest ✍ **8**

Visit our Web site at http://www.mathleague.com

Solutions on Page 95 • Answers on Page 143

2002-2003 Annual 8th Grade Contest

Tuesday, February 18 or 25, 2003

Instructions

8

- **Time** You will have only *30 minutes* working time for this contest. You might be *unable* to finish all 40 questions in the time allowed.

- **Scores** Please remember that *this is a contest, not a test*—and there is no "passing" or "failing" score. Few students score as high as 30 points (75% correct). Students with half that, 15 points, *should be commended!*

- **Format and Point Value** This is a multiple-choice contest. Each answer is an A, B, C, or D. Write each answer in the *Answers* column to the right of each question. A correct answer is worth 1 point. Unanswered questions get no credit. You **may** use a calculator.

1. Round 0.0409 to the nearest hundredth.

   A) 0.0401   B) 0.040   C) 0.041   D) 0.04

   1.

2. The sum of 0.5 and its reciprocal is

   A) 0   B) 1   C) 2   D) 2.5

   2.

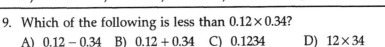

3. I ate as many doughnuts as there are digits in the product $2\,000\,000 \times 5\,000\,000$ that are *not* 0. How many doughnuts did I eat?

   A) 1   B) 2   C) 7   D) 10

   3.

4. Which is the only integer whose square is less than its double?

   A) 2   B) 1   C) 0   D) –2

   4.

5. $25 \times \left(\frac{1}{4} + \frac{1}{4} + \frac{1}{4} + \frac{1}{4}\right) =$ A) 0.25 B) 1 C) 25 D) 100

   5.

6. The largest odd factor of 210 is

   A) 21   B) 63   C) 105   D) 209

   6.

7. $(111 - 11) \times (1111 - 111) = 100 \times \underline{\ ?\ }$

   A) 10   B) 11   C) 100   D) 1000

   7.

8. Asked on Tues., "Did you saw your wife?," a magician said, "Yes, I did so 31 days ago, on a

   A) Thurs.   B) Fri.   C) Sat.   D) Sun.

   8.

9. Which of the following is less than 0.12×0.34?

   A) $0.12 - 0.34$ B) $0.12 + 0.34$ C) 0.1234   D) 12×34

   9.

10. $7 + 8 \times 7 + 8 =$

    A) $(7+8) \times 7 + 8$ B) $7 + (8 \times 7) + 8$ C) $7 + 8 \times (7+8)$ D) $(7+8) \times (7+8)$

    10.

11. A right triangle can have at most $\underline{\ ?\ }$ of length 5.

    A) 3 sides   B) 2 sides   C) 1 side   D) 0 sides

    11.

12. Under the couch, I found 100 dollars + 100 quarters + 100 dimes + 100 nickels. I found a total of

    A) $140   B) $145   C) $175   D) $400

    12.

13. $121\,212\,121\,212 \div 3 = 363\,636\,363\,636 \div \underline{\ ?\ }$

    A) 1   B) 6   C) 9   D) 27

    13.

14. All of the following equal one-half *except*

    A) $\left(\frac{1}{4}\right)^2$ B) $\frac{60}{120}$ C) 0.5   D) $\sqrt{\frac{1}{4}}$

    14.

Go on to the next page ⫸ **8**

32

15. $\frac{1}{3} \times 9 \times \frac{1}{6} \times 6 \times \frac{1}{9} \times 3 =$ A) 9 B) 3 C) 1 D) $\frac{1}{6}$ | 15.

16. The sum of four numbers is one-half. Their average is | 16.
    A) one-eighth B) one-fourth C) one-half   D) 2

17. The front of my hat is an isosceles triangle, two of | 17.
    whose sides are 12 and 24. The triangle's perimeter is
    A) 36   B) 42   C) 60   D) 72

18. Factor $6 \times 12 \times 18 \times 24$ into primes. | 18.
    A) $2^6 \times 3^6$ B) $2^7 \times 3^6$ C) $2^6 \times 3^5$ D) $2^7 \times 3^5$

19. 20% of 30 = 30% of _?_   A) 0.2 B) 20 C) 2% D) 200% | 19.

20. Multiplying 7 by 0.25 gets the same result as dividing 7 by | 20.
    A) 0.25   B) 4   C) 25   D) 100

21. Every _?_ number is divisible by at least one prime. | 21.
    A) whole   B) odd   C) even   D) positive

22. Ann is older than Bob and younger | 22.
    than Sue. If Dan is older than Ann,
    who could be the same age?
    A) Bob & Sue   B) Dan & Bob
    C) Ann & Bob   D) Sue & Dan

23. The number $(0.1)^{10}$ is equal to | 23.
    A) 1   B) $\frac{1}{10}$ C) $\frac{1}{100}$ D) $\frac{1}{10^{10}}$

24. A 139-minute movie starts at 8:30 P.M. At what time will it end? | 24.
    A) 10:39 P.M.   B) 10:49 P.M.   C) 10:59 P.M.   D) 11:19 P.M.

25. $\frac{2^2}{4^2} + \frac{4^2}{2^2} = 2^2 +$ _?_   A) $\frac{1}{2^2}$ B) 0 C) 2^2 D) 4^2 | 25.

26. 10% = _?_ ÷ 10   A) 1 B) 10 C) 100 D) 10 000 | 26.

27. If 24 kittens weigh the same as 18 puppies, then 24 puppies | 27.
    weigh the same as _?_ kittens.
    A) 18   B) 24   C) 32   D) 36

28. If I add the digits of my phone's extension num- | 28.
    ber, I get 28. That number can't have _?_ digits.
    A) 3   B) 4   C) 5   D) 7

Go on to the next page ⏵ **8**

33

29. $\frac{3}{4} : 3 = \frac{4}{3} : \underline{\ ?\ }$ A) $\frac{9}{4}$ B) $\frac{16}{3}$ C) 4   D) 12 | 29.

30. The product of a number and its additive inverse *never* equals | 30.

     A) 0   B) –1   C) 1   D) –4

31. In 8 crow's nests, 15 crows nested either alone or paired with only one other crow. How many of the 15 crows nested alone? | 31.

     A) 0   B) 1   C) 2   D) 3

32. What is the smallest possible difference between the sum of five consecutive positive integers and the largest of them? | 32.

     A) 0   B) 2   C) 5   D) 10

33. $2^2 \times 2^4 = 2 \times \underline{\ ?\ }$ | 33.

     A) 2^5 B) 2^6 C) 2^7 D) 2^8

34. If I read 90 pages per hour, how many 270-page books can I read in 6 hours? | 34.

     A) 2   B) 3   C) 15   D) 18

35. A *perfect square* is the product of any integer and itself. How many perfect squares are factors of $2 \times 4 \times 6 \times 8 \times 10$? | 35.

     A) 5   B) 4   C) 3   D) 2

36. If the circumference of a circle is 4 cm, its area is $\underline{\ ?\ }$ cm^2. | 36.

     A) $\frac{4}{\pi}$ B) $\frac{16}{\pi}$ C) 4π D) 16π

37. If two sides of a right triangle are 3 and 5, then the triangle's perimeter could be | 37.

     A) 10   B) 11   C) 12   D) 13

38. If each face of a Jack-in-the-Box cube has a perimeter of 36, the cube's volume is | 38.

     A) 36   B) 81   C) 216   D) 729

39. If n is a whole number, which of the following could equal n^3? | 39.

     A) 2.7×10^{27} B) 2.7×10^{28} C) 2.7×10^{29} D) 2.7×10^{30}

40. Which of the following could possibly be the sum of all the integers in a set of 1000 consecutive positive integers? | 40.

     A) 499 000   B) 499 500   C) 500 000   D) 500 500

The end of the contest 🖎 **8**

Visit our Web site at http://www.mathleague.com

Solutions on Page 99 • Answers on Page 144

2003-2004 Annual 8th Grade Contest

Tuesday, February 17 or 24, 2004

Instructions

8

- **Time** You will have only *30 minutes* working time for this contest. You might be *unable* to finish all 40 questions in the time allowed.

- **Scores** Please remember that *this is a contest, not a test*—and there is no "passing" or "failing" score. Few students score as high as 30 points (75% correct). Students with half that, 15 points, *should be commended!*

- **Format and Point Value** This is a multiple-choice contest. Each answer is an A, B, C, or D. Write each answer in the *Answers* column to the right of each question. A correct answer is worth 1 point. Unanswered questions get no credit. You **may** use a calculator.

1. $(99-98) \times (88-87) \times (77-76) \times (66-65) =$ A) 0 B) 1 C) 4 D) 11	1.
2. $1^2 + (-1)^2 - 1^2 =$ A) 1 B) –1 C) 0 D) 3	2.
3. The base of my panic button is a square with an even perimeter. It can't have a side of length A) 0.50 B) 0.75 C) 1.00 D) 1.50 	3.
4. $21+28+35+42+49+56+63 = 7 \times \underline{?}$ A) 7 B) 14 C) 42 D) 49	4.
5. $\frac{3}{12} = \frac{?}{16}$ A) 4 B) 3 C) $\frac{1}{4}$ D) 25%	5.
6. Which type of triangle has the largest angle? A) equilateral B) acute C) obtuse D) right	6.
7. A CD costs 30 quarters, 30 dimes, 30 nickels, and 30 pennies. If I pay with 30 half-dollars, I will have overpaid by A) \$2.30 B) \$2.70 C) \$3.00 D) \$3.20	7.
8. If I have \$39.99, I can buy *at most* <u> ? </u> 39¢ trinkets. A) 100 B) 101 C) 102 D) 103	8.
9. What is the tens' digit of the product 8765×4321? A) 5 B) 6 C) 7 D) 8	9.
10. How many grains of rice are in 1 kg of my famous rice if the average weight of 1 grain of my rice is 0.01 g? A) 100 B) 1000 C) 10 000 D) 100 000 	10.
11. $120 \div 2 = 180 \div 3 = 240 \div 4 = 360 \div \underline{?}$ A) 5 B) 6 C) 8 D) 12	11.
12. The additive inverse of $\frac{1}{2}$ is a <u> ? </u> number. A) negative B) whole C) prime D) positive 	12.
13. Kay has an ice cream sundae every Sunday in May. If May 1 is a Saturday, then exactly how many sundaes will Kay have in May? A) 2 B) 3 C) 4 D) 5	13.
14. The sum of two odd numbers cannot equal A) 124 B) 142 C) 214 D) 241	14.
15. If twice a certain number is 96, then one-third of the number is A) 16 B) 32 C) 48 D) 64	15.

Go on to the next page ⫸ **8**

16. Of the following, which pair has the greatest common factor?

    A) 33, 90   B) 36, 63   C) 66, 96   D) 99, 39

16.

17. If each of 5 numbers is increased by 10% of its value, then the sum of the 5 numbers is increased by _?_% of its value.

    A) 1   B) 2   C) 10   D) 50

17.

18. At 2 PM I'll begin to draw 32 3-minute pencil sketches. I'll rest 2 minutes between sketches, so I'll finish the sketches at _?_ PM.

    A) 4:37   B) 4:38   C) 4:39   D) 4:40

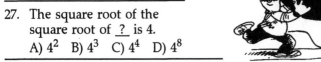

18.

19. 3 minutes = _?_% of 90 minutes.

    A) $\frac{1}{3}$ B) $\frac{1}{2}$ C) $\frac{10}{3}$ D) 5

19.

20. $(100 + 88) \times (100 - 88) =$

    A) 0   B) 100^2 C) 2×8800 D) $100^2 - 88^2$

20.

21. In 30 years, my current age will triple. How old am I now?

    A) 15   B) 12   C) 10   D) 9

21.

22. What is the smallest positive integer that is a multiple of $\frac{38}{57}$?

    A) 2   B) 19   C) 38   D) 57

22.

23. Of the following numbers, which has the greatest value?

    A) 1^{25} B) 25%   C) $\frac{1}{25}$ D) 2.5

23.

24. If $AB + BC = 18$, then the perimeter of $\triangle ABC$ *cannot* equal

    A) 33   B) 34   C) 35   D) 36

24.

25. You add 100 different positive integers. I add 99 of these 100. The least possible difference between your sum and mine is

    A) 0   B) 1   C) 99   D) 100

25.

26. A ball with a 5 m circumference needs _?_ turns to roll 1 km in a straight line.

    A) 400   B) 314
    C) 200   D) 100

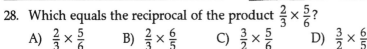

26.

27. The square root of the square root of _?_ is 4.

    A) 4^2 B) 4^3 C) 4^4 D) 4^8

27.

28. Which equals the reciprocal of the product $\frac{2}{3} \times \frac{5}{6}$?

    A) $\frac{2}{3} \times \frac{5}{6}$ B) $\frac{2}{3} \times \frac{6}{5}$ C) $\frac{3}{2} \times \frac{5}{6}$ D) $\frac{3}{2} \times \frac{6}{5}$

28.

29. The least possible sum of 5 different positive multiples of 6 is

    A) 60   B) 90   C) 130   D) 160

29.

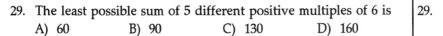

Go on to the next page ▌▌▶ **8**

30. If a certain two-digit number is equal to twice the sum of its digits, what is the sum of its digits?

A) 9   B) 12   C) 18   D) 36

30.

31. The *distance* between steps on a ladder is measured from the top of a step to the bottom of a higher step. If the distance between adjacent steps of my ladder is 25 cm, and each step is 2 cm thick, what is the distance between step 1 and step 7?

A) 135 cm   B) 137 cm   C) 160 cm   D) 162 cm

31.

32. If the average of three *different* positive integers is 3, their least possible product is

A) 9   B) 12   C) 24   D) 27

32.

33. If *abcd* = $a \times d + b \times c$, then *2543* =

A) 14   B) 22   C) 26   D) 120

33.

34. If the sum of two positive integers is divided by their difference, a possible value of the quotient is

A) 0   B) 0.5   C) 1   D) 2

34.

35. (# of minutes in a second) ÷ (# of seconds in a minute) is

A) 3600   B) 60   C) 1   D) less than 1

35.

36. The number $\frac{1}{111}$ is _?_ % of the number 111 (to the nearest 0.001%).

A) 0.008%   B) 0.009%   C) 0.901%   D) 1.000%

36.

37. $\sqrt{\sqrt{9^{16}}}$ =   A) 3^2 B) 9^2 C) 9^4 D) 9^8

37.

38. Today, Grandma rode 20% further than she rode on Sunday, in 20% less time than Sunday's ride took. Her speed today was _?_ % of her speed on Sunday.

A) 140   B) 150   C) 160   D) 170

38.

39. Grandma is 100. Her age in months contained two more digits than her age in years during all *or part* of _?_ of those 100 years.

A) 16   B) 17   C) 18   D) 19

39.

40. What is the difference between the sum of the first 2004 positive integers and the sum of the next 2004 positive integers?

A) 2004   B) 4008   C) 2004^2 D) 4008^2

40.

The end of the contest 👉 **8**

Visit our Web site at http://www.mathleague.com
Solutions on Page 103 • Answers on Page 145

38

2004-2005 Annual 8th Grade Contest

February 15 or 22, 2005

Instructions

8

- **Time** You will have only *30 minutes* working time for this contest. You might be *unable* to finish all 40 questions in the time allowed.

- **Scores** Please remember that *this is a contest, not a test*—and there is no "passing" or "failing" score. Few students score as high as 30 points (75% correct). Students with half that, 15 points, *should be commended!*

- **Format and Point Value** This is a multiple-choice contest. Each answer is an A, B, C, or D. Write each answer in the *Answers* column to the right of each question. A correct answer is worth 1 point. Unanswered questions get no credit. You **may** use a calculator.

1. $1110 - 1020 = 110 - \underline{\ ?\ }$ A) 102   B) 101   C) 90   D) 20 | 1.

2. If my doctor's "**IN**" sign is a square with a perimeter of 4, then its area is
   A) 1   B) 4   C) 8   D) 16 | 2.

3. $300 \div 200 = 1 \div \underline{\ ?\ }$ | 3.
   A) $\frac{1}{3}$ B) $\frac{1}{2}$ C) $\frac{2}{3}$ D) $\frac{3}{2}$

4. When written as an improper fraction, five-fourths is | 4.
   A) $\frac{4}{5}$ B) $1\frac{1}{4}$ C) 1.25   D) $\frac{5}{4}$

5. $2005 - 2005 - 2004 =$ A) 1   B) –2004   C) –2005   D) –2006 | 5.

6. Exactly 120 seconds after midnight, the correct time is | 6.
   A) 12:02 P.M.   B) 12:02 A.M.   C) 2 P.M.   D) 2 A.M.

7. $24 \div 4 \times 2 + 4 =$ | 7.
   A) 1   B) 7   C) 16   D) 36

8. The reciprocal of $(\frac{1}{2} \times 4)$ is | 8.
   A) $2 \times \frac{1}{4}$ B) $\frac{1}{2} \times 4$ C) $\frac{1}{2} \times \frac{1}{4}$ D) 2×4

9. Of the following numbers, which is closest in value to 1? | 9.
   A) 0.995   B) 0.99   C) 1.01   D) 1.1

10. What is the sum of all the one-digit positive prime numbers? | 10.
    A) 15   B) 16   C) 17   D) 18

11. $2 \times \frac{1}{2} \times 4 \times \frac{1}{4} \times 6 \times \frac{1}{6} =$ | 11.
    A) 1   B) 6   C) 12   D) 24

12. When I add the measures of *any* 2 angles of triangle *T*, the sum is always 120°. Triangle *T must* be | 12.
    A) scalene   B) right   C) obtuse   D) equiangular

13. I wear my headphones only on cloudy days. The day after each cloudy day is a sunny day. I wear my headphones at most $\underline{\ ?\ }$ times in a week. | 13.
    A) 3   B) 4   C) 5   D) 6

14. Of the following, which has the largest value? | 14.
    A) 7   B) $(-1)^2$ C) $(-2)^2$ D) $(-3)^2$

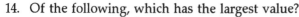
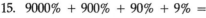

15. $9000\% + 900\% + 90\% + 9\% =$ | 15.
    A) 9999   B) 999.9   C) 99.99   D) 0.9999

Go on to the next page ⫸ **8**

16. A dealer paid Bunny Fabergé 50 pennies for each of his decorated eggs, The dealer then sold each egg for 50 quarters. Bunny (the artist) got what percent of the final purchase price?

    A) 2%   B) 4%   C) 25%   D) 50%

16.

17. $\sqrt{\sqrt{\sqrt{256}}} =$

    A) 2   B) 4   C) 8   D) 16

17.

18. $30\% \times 40\% =$ A) 12% B) 120% C) 1200% D) 12000%

18.

19. The number _?_ has exactly 4 different whole number factors.

    A) 30   B) 24   C) 12   D) 10

19.

20. When rounded to the nearest *fifth*, 0.33 becomes

    A) 0.2   B) 0.3   C) $\frac{2}{5}$ D) $\frac{3}{5}$

20.

21. I lost my coins! This morning, I had 7 coins worth 49¢. How many nickels did I have?

    A) 0   B) 1   C) 2   D) 7

21.

22. 1.5 m + 60 cm + 0.02 km =

    A) 0.221 m B) 2.21 m C) 22.1 m D) 221 m

22.

23. How many of the positive multiples of 2 are factors of 222?

    A) 111   B) 4   C) 3   D) 1

23.

24. What is the average of the first 99 positive whole numbers?

    A) 49.00   B) 49.50   C) 49.75   D) 50.00

24.

25. If a small circle's diameter is a large circle's radius, then the small circle's area is _?_ % of the large circle's area.

    A) 20   B) 25   C) 40   D) 50

25.

26. If 2/3 of a cup of fish food can feed 8 goldfish, then 4 cups of fish food should be able to feed _?_ goldfish.

    A) 12   B) 24   C) 36   D) 48

26.

27. An integer *cannot* be _?_ if its square is even.

    A) prime   B) odd   C) even   D) zero

27.

28. If $4x =$ the reciprocal of $\frac{1}{x^3}$, then x could equal

    A) $\frac{1}{8}$ B) $\frac{1}{2}$ C) 2   D) 8

28.

Go on to the next page ⫸ **8**

29. $2^{10} \times 2^{10} =$ A) 2^{20} B) 2^{100} C) 4^{20} D) 4^{100} | 29.

30. I got immunized on the one millionth second of this calendar year. That happened on
A) January 11   B) January 12
C) February 1   D) February 2 | 30.

31. $\sqrt{16^{16}} =$
A) 4^4 B) 4^8 C) 16^4 D) 16^8 | 31.

32. Each of 2005 fractions has an even numerator and an odd denominator. If the product of all of them is an integer, it must be
A) even   B) odd   C) prime   D) 2005 | 32.

33. If x is a whole number, what is the largest possible perimeter of a triangle with side-lengths 3, 4, and x?
A) 11   B) 12   C) 13   D) 14 | 33.

34. When fully expanded, $10\,000^{9999}$ has ? digits.
A) 9999   B) 10 000   C) 39 996   D) 39 997 | 34.

35. In the diagram, the total number of different triangles is
A) 2   B) 3   C) 4   D) 5 | 35.

36. If the sum of 2000 consecutive integers is 1000, then the sum of the digits of the *greatest* of these 2000 integers is
A) 1   B) 2   C) 9   D) 27 | 36.

37. How many of the 15 positive factors of 400 are divisible by 4?
A) 4   B) 8   C) 9   D) 10 | 37.

38. I phoned my mom to help me answer this, the final question on a quiz show: *How many integers equal their own squares?* Mom said, " ? ." She was right!
A) zero   B) one
C) two   D) three | 38.

39. At 12:22, a clock's hour hand is ? away from a vertical position.
A) 10°   B) 11°   C) 21°   D) 22° | 39.

40. What is the tens' digit of the product $1 \times 2 \times 3 \times \ldots \times 98 \times 99$?
A) 4   B) 6   C) 8   D) 0 | 40.

The end of the contest **8**

Visit our Web site at http://www.mathleague.com

Solutions on Page 107 • Answers on Page 146

42

2005-2006 Annual 8th Grade Contest

February 21 or 28, 2006

Instructions

8

- **Time** You will have only *30 minutes* working time for this contest. You might be *unable* to finish all 40 questions in the time allowed.

- **Scores** Please remember that *this is a contest, not a test*—and there is no "passing" or "failing" score. Few students score as high as 30 points (75% correct). Students with half that, 15 points, *should be commended!*

- **Format and Point Value** This is a multiple-choice contest. Each answer is an A, B, C, or D. Write each answer in the *Answers* column to the right of each question. A correct answer is worth 1 point. Unanswered questions get no credit. You **may** use a calculator.

1. $11\,011 = 1001 + \underline{\ ?\ }$
   A) 1001   B) 10\,001   C) 10\,010   D) 10\,101

1.

2. Earth is the 5th largest of 9 planets. The ratio of the number of planets larger than Earth to the number smaller than Earth is
   A) 1:1   B) 2:1   C) 4:5   D) 5:4

2.

3. Of the following, which is the product of 2 consecutive integers?
   A) 65   B) 80   C) 96   D) 110

3.

4. Two perpendicular lines intersect in exactly
   A) 0 points   B) 1 point   C) 2 points   D) 4 points

4.

5. The prime factorization of 40 is
   A) 2×20 B) $2 \times 2 \times 10$ C) $2 \times 4 \times 5$ D) $2 \times 2 \times 2 \times 5$

5.

6. $\underline{\ ?\ }$ is *not* the sum of a positive integer and its reciprocal.
   A) $12\frac{1}{12}$ B) $6\frac{2}{12}$ C) $4\frac{4}{12}$ D) $2\frac{6}{12}$

6.

7. $\frac{1}{2} \times \frac{1}{2} = \frac{1}{2} \div \underline{\ ?\ }$ A) 4   B) 2   C) $\frac{1}{2}$ D) $\frac{1}{4}$

7.

8. What is the least number of acute angles possible in a triangle?
   A) 0   B) 1   C) 2   D) 3

8.

9. $0.5 \times 0.5 = 0.25 \times \underline{\ ?\ }$
   A) 1   B) 0.75
   C) 0.25   D) 10

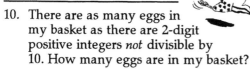

9.

10. There are as many eggs in my basket as there are 2-digit positive integers *not* divisible by 10. How many eggs are in my basket?
    A) 78   B) 79   C) 80   D) 81

10.

11. $3^2 + 3^2 = 6^2 - \underline{\ ?\ }$
    A) 2^2 B) 3^2 C) $2^2 + 2^2$ D) $3^2 + 3^2$

11.

12. The product of two even numbers is *not* always divisible by
    A) 1   B) 2   C) 4   D) 8

12.

13. I need $\underline{\ ?\ }$ 4×6 photos to completely fill a 24×40 display board.
    A) 40   B) 24   C) 20   D) 16

13.

14. $\frac{2}{3} + \frac{3}{2} + \frac{2}{3} + \frac{3}{2} + \frac{2}{3} =$
    A) $3+2$ B) $3-2$ C) $3 \div 2$ D) $2 \div 3$

14.

Go on to the next page ⫸ **8**

15. Of the following, which is the *least*?   15.
    A) $(1+1) \div (1 \times 1) - 1$ B) $1 + (1 \div 1 \times 1) - 1$
    C) $1 + (1 \div 1 \times 1 - 1)$ D) $(1 + 1 \div 1) \times (1 - 1)$

16. What is the average of 10, –10, 5, –5, and 100?   16.
    A) 0   B) 20   C) 25   D) 100

17. I cut a string 40 m long into 4 equal pieces and formed a rectangle   17.
    from 1 piece. The sum of the width and length of my rectangle was
    A) 5 m   B) 10 m   C) 20 m   D) 40 m

18. The ones' digit of the product of 2 consecutive integers *could* be   18.
    A) 1   B) 2   C) 3   D) 4

19. Righty's drink is 36% soy milk.   19.
    Lefty's is 4% soy milk. If equal
    amounts of each are mixed, the result-
    ing mixture would be _?_ % soy milk.
    A) 20   B) 32   C) 36   D) 40

20. The least common multiple of 8, 12, and 20 is   20.
    A) 40   B) 60   C) 120   D) 1920

21. Of the following, which is a multiple of 7?   21.
    A) 749 775   B) 735 814   C) 784 284   D) 770 357

22. $\sqrt{2} \times \sqrt{4} \times \sqrt{6} \times \sqrt{8} = \underline{\ ?\ } \times \sqrt{1} \times \sqrt{2} \times \sqrt{3} \times \sqrt{4}$ 22.
    A) $\sqrt{2}$ B) 2   C) 4   D) 16

23. The average of eight numbers is 0. Their sum must   23.
    A) equal 0   B) equal 1   C) exceed 0   D) be negative

24. There are as many seconds in 1 hour as there are minutes in   24.
    A) 24 hours   B) 30 hours   C) 60 hours   D) 90 hours

25. _?_ is more than 3 times as many days before July 1 as it is after May 1.   25.
    A) May 16   B) May 17   C) June 15   D) June 16

26. Of 30 veggies, if 20 were   26.
    sliced, then 18 were diced,
    then *at most* _?_ were
    neither sliced nor diced.
    A) 2   B) 8   C) 10   D) 12

27. 40% of _?_ is 80.   27.
    A) 32   B) 120   C) 180   D) 200

28. $(\frac{7}{8})^7 \div (\frac{8}{7})^8 =$ 28.
    A) 1   B) $\frac{7}{8}$ C) $(\frac{7}{8})^{15}$ D) $(\frac{7}{8})^{56}$

Go on to the next page ⫸ **8**

29. The product of two consecutive integers is always

    A) even   B) odd   C) positive   D) divisible by 6

    29.

30. To the nearest 1%, the circumference of a circle with diameter 2 is _?_% of the perimeter of a square with side-length 2.

    A) 75%   B) 76%   C) 78%   D) 79%

    30.

31. I read a 300-page book in 4.5 hours. If I took at least 30 seconds to read every page, then I read the first 100 pages in *at most*

    A) 50 minutes   B) 170 minutes   C) 180 minutes   D) 200 minutes

    31.

32. Semicircles are drawn on opposite sides of a 2×2 square, as shown. What is the perimeter of the shaded region?

    A) $4+2\pi$ B) $8+2\pi$ C) $4+\pi$ D) $4-\pi$

    32.

33. What is the smallest of 20 consecutive primes whose sum is 639?

    A) 5   B) 3   C) 2   D) 1

    33.

34. I quadrupled the area of a 1×6 rectangular APPLAUSE sign, but left the ratio of its side-lengths unchanged. The perimeter of the new sign is

    APPLAUSE!

    A) 24   B) 28   C) 48   D) 56

    34.

35. $\sqrt{1\%} =$

    A) $\frac{1}{2}\%$ B) 1%   C) 10%   D) 100%

    35.

36. How many different positive integers are factors of 3^6?

    A) 3   B) 6   C) 7   D) 18

    36.

37. Every hour, the second hand of a circular clock moves a total of

    A) 60°   B) 360°   C) 3600°   D) 21 600°

    37.

38. The positive-integer factors of _?_ have an average value of 2.

    A) 3   B) 4   C) 6   D) 8

    38.

39. If the marks on the number line are equally spaced, what is the average of the numbers at points A and B?

    A) $\frac{1}{12}$ B) $\frac{1}{6}$ C) $\frac{1}{5}$ D) $\frac{2}{15}$

    39.

40. The sum of the first 2006 positive odd integers is

    A) 2×1003^2 B) $2^2 \times 1003^2$ C) 5×1003^2 D) 6×1003^2

    40.

The end of the contest 🖎 **8**

Solutions on Page 111 • Answers on Page 147

Algebra Course 1 Contests

2001-2002 through 2005-2006

2001-2002 Annual Algebra Course 1 Contest

Spring, 2002

Instructions

■ **Time** You will have only *30 minutes* working time for this contest. You might be *unable* to finish all 30 questions in the time allowed.

■ **Scores** Please remember that *this is a contest, not a test*—and there is no "passing" or "failing" score. Few students score as high as 24 points (80% correct). Students with half that, 12 points, *deserve commendation!*

■ **Format and Point Value** This is a multiple-choice contest. Each answer is an A, B, C, or D. Write each answer in the *Answer Column* to the right of each question. A correct answer is worth 1 point. Unanswered questions get no credit. You **may** use a calculator.

1. If $x+2002 = 2001$, then $x =$

   A) –1   B) 1   C) –2003   D) 2003

1.

2. Which number is 50% greater than x?

   A) $0.5x$ B) $\frac{x}{2}$ C) $1.5x$ D) $150x$

2.

3. I watched 1000 ants build an anthill in 5 hours. Working at the same rate, 2500 ants could have built the anthill in _?_ hours.

   A) 1   B) 2   C) 3   D) 4

3.

4. If n is the number of primes less than 50, then _?_ is the number of primes less than 60.

   A) $n+1$ B) $n+2$ C) $n+3$ D) $n+4$

4.

5. If the average (arithmetic mean) of x, y, and z is 18, then $x+y+z =$

   A) 6   B) 18   C) 36   D) 54

5.

6. The result of adding a number to itself is usually *unequal* to the result of multiplying the number by itself. For how many different numbers are these results equal?

   A) none B) one   C) two   D) four

6.

7. $(x+1)^2 - (x-1)^2 =$

   A) 2   B) –2   C) $4x$ D) $-4x$

7.

8. If $\sqrt{4} + \sqrt{x} = \sqrt{16}$, then $x =$

   A) 2   B) 4   C) 8   D) 12

8.

9. The side-lengths of quadrilateral Q are consecutive integers. If Q's perimeter is 8014, how long is Q's longest side?

   A) 2002 B) 2003 C) 2004 D) 2005

9.

10. The square roots of Pat's and Lee's ages have a sum of 7 and a difference of 1. If Pat is older than Lee, how old is Pat?

    A) 3   B) 4   C) 9   D) 16

10.

Go on to the next page ▌▌▶ **A**

11. If $(x-1)(x-2) = 6$, then $(1-x)(2-x) =$

    A) -6 B) -36 C) 6 D) 36

11.

12. A straight line through the origin and (a,b) also passes through

    A) $(-a,b)$ B) $(a,-b)$
    C) $(-a,-b)$ D) (a^2,b^2)

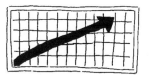

12.

13. What is the product of all the even numbers that are both greater than -10 and less than $+10$?

    A) $38\,400^2$ B) 384^2 C) 384 D) 0

13.

14. If a line whose x- and y-intercepts are equal does *not* pass through the origin, then its slope must be

    A) 0 B) 1 C) -1 D) undefined

14.

15. The least common multiple of $4x^4$ and $6x^6$ is

    A) $2x^4$ B) $12x^6$ C) $12x^{12}$ D) $24x^{24}$

15.

16. $\pi(\pi^2+\pi) + \pi(\pi^2-\pi) =$

    A) 0 B) π^3 C) $2\pi^3$ D) $2\pi^3+2\pi^2$

16.

17. If the roots of $ax^2+bx+c = 0$ are 6 and 9, then the roots of $3ax^2+3bx+3c = 0$ are

    A) 2 and 3   B) 6 and 9   C) 18 and 27   D) -2 and -3

17.

18. What percent of $0.5p$ is p?

    A) $(1/2)\%$ B) 20% C) 50% D) 200%

18.

19. Exactly _?_ different pairs of integers (x,y) represent points on the circle $x^2+y^2 = 25$.

    A) twelve   B) eight   C) six   D) four

19.

20. If $(17.6x)^3 = 7883$, then $(1.76x)^3 =$

    A) 788.3   B) 78.83   C) 7.883   D) 0.7883

20.

21. For how many different positive integers n will n, $n+2$, and $n+4$ represent three different prime numbers?

    A) none   B) one   C) two   D) three

21.

Go on to the next page ⮕ **A**

22. The reciprocal of 4 equals the average of the reciprocals of 3 and

    A) 5   B) 6   C) $\frac{1}{5}$ D) $\frac{1}{6}$

    22.

23. When each letter in the phrase "my huge taco" is replaced by a different digit, the value of $m+y+h+u+g+e+t+a+c+o$ will be

    A) 9   B) 10   C) 45   D) 55

    23.

24. If $x \geq 100$, then $\sqrt{x+16}$ is between

    A) $\sqrt{x}$ and $\sqrt{x}+1$ B) $\sqrt{x}+1$ and $\sqrt{x}+2$
    C) $\sqrt{x}+2$ and $\sqrt{x}+3$ D) $\sqrt{x}+3$ and $\sqrt{x}+4$

    24.

25. $\frac{1}{1\times 2} + \frac{1}{2\times 3} + \frac{1}{3\times 4} + \ldots + \frac{1}{2000\times 2001} + \frac{1}{2001\times 2002} =$

    A) $\frac{1}{2002}$ B) $\frac{1999}{2002}$ C) $\frac{2001}{2002}$ D) 1

    25.

26. Add all 100 roots of $(x+1)(x-2)(x+3)\times\ldots\times(x-98)(x+99)(x-100) = 0$.

    A) 100   B) 50   C) –50   D) –100

    26.

27. If $|x| = -y$, then it is *always* true that $|y| =$

    A) x B) $-x$ C) y D) $-y$

    27.

28. No matter what two integers I choose, their squares *cannot* differ by

    A) 2002   B) 2003   C) 2004   D) 2005

    28.

29. If I run my first 60 km lap at a rate 25% faster than my usual 12 km/hr, and my second 60 km lap at a rate _?_ % slower than 12 km/hr, then my overall average speed will be my usual speed.

    A) $\frac{50}{3}$ B) 20   C) 25   D) $\frac{250}{3}$

    29.

30. To get a year's *digit-product*, multiply the year's digits. For example, between 1900 and 2000, the 2 years 1913 and 1931 each have a digit-product of 27. What is the largest integer n for which n of the years from 1900–2000 have the same non-zero digit-product?

    A) 2   B) 3   C) 4   D) 6

    30.

The end of the contest **A**

Visit our Web site at http://www.mathleague.com

Solutions on Page 117 • Answers on Page 148

2002-2003 Annual Algebra Course 1 Contest

Spring, 2003

Instructions

- **Time** You will have only *30 minutes* working time for this contest. You might be *unable* to finish all 30 questions in the time allowed.

- **Scores** Please remember that *this is a contest, not a test*—and there is no "passing" or "failing" score. Few students score as high as 24 points (80% correct). Students with half that, 12 points, *deserve commendation!*

- **Format and Point Value** This is a multiple-choice contest. Each answer is an A, B, C, or D. Write each answer in the *Answer Column* to the right of each question. A correct answer is worth 1 point. Unanswered questions get no credit. You **may** use a calculator.

1. If $x = 10$, then $2x^3 + 0x^2 + 0x + 3 =$

   A) 23   B) 203   C) 230   D) 2003

   1.

2. Each of the following is a factor of x^2+3x-4 *except*

   A) $x+4$ B) $x-1$ C) $x-4$ D) 1

   2.

3. If $(n)(2003) = 2003 + 2003 + 2003 + 2003 + 2003$, then $n =$

   A) 5   B) 2001   C) 2002   D) 2003

   3.

4. The least value of x for which $\frac{2}{x}$ is an integer is

   A) -2   B) 2   C) -1   D) 1

   4.

5. My party hat, when unfolded, is a *square*. When the area of this square is divided by its perimeter, the quotient is 4. How long is a side of this square?

   A) 4   B) 8   C) 16   D) 64

   5.

6. $(x+1) - (x-1) + (2+x) - (2-x) =$

   A) $2x$ B) $2x+2$ C) 2   D) 6

   6.

7. The number of even integers between 1 and 2003 is the same as the number of odd integers between 4 and

   A) 2000   B) 2002   C) 2004   D) 2006

   7.

8. If $\frac{2001}{x} + \frac{2002}{x} + \frac{2003}{x} = 1$, then $x =$

   A) 6002   B) 6004   C) 6006   D) 6008

   8.

9. What is the area of a triangle whose vertices have coordinates (1,1), (11,1), and (1,11)?

   A) 50   B) 60.5   C) 100   D) 121

   9.

10. If the letters s, t, o, and p each represent a different positive odd integer, what is the least possible value of $\sqrt{s+t+o+p}$?

    A) 2   B) 4   C) 8   D) 16

    10.

11. If y is positive, then the square root of the square root of the square root of ? is y.

    A) y^3 B) y^6 C) y^8 D) y^{16}

    11.

Go on to the next page ⫸ **A**

12. The least possible sum of a positive number and its reciprocal is | 12.

    A) 1   B) 1.5   C) 2   D) 2.5

13. $(x^2 + y^2)^2 = x^4 + \underline{\ ?\ } + y^4$ | 13.

    A) xy B) $2xy$ C) x^2y^2 D) $2x^2y^2$

14. There is no positive value of $x < 1$ for which x^{1000} can equal | 14.

    A) $\frac{1}{\pi}$ B) $\frac{2}{\pi}$ C) $\frac{3}{\pi}$ D) $\frac{4}{\pi}$

15. $5^{2003} \div (-5)^{2002} =$ | 15.

    A) 1   B) 5   C) –1   D) –5

16. The square of the sum of 3 consecutive integers must be divisible by | 16.

    A) 2   B) 4   C) 9   D) 16

17. Which of the following points is *not* on the line $y = \pi x + \pi$? | 17.

    A) $(-1,0)$ B) $(0,\pi)$ C) $(0,-1)$ D) $(1,2\pi)$

18. For a canned food drive, I rounded up canned corned beef and canned tomato soup. The number of cans of corned beef was 25% of the number of cans of soup. The number of cans of soup was $\underline{\ ?\ }$% of the total number of these cans. | 18.

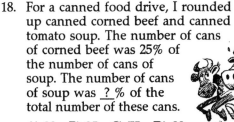

    A) 20   B) 25   C) 75   D) 80

19. $(x-1)^3(x+1)^2 =$ | 19.

    A) $(x-1)(x^2-1)^2$ B) $(x-1)(x^2+1)^2$

    C) $(x+1)(x^2-1)^2$ D) $(x+1)(x^2+1)^2$

20. If $(x+y-17)^2 = 0$ and $(x-y-13)^2 = 0$, then $y =$ | 20.

    A) 2   B) 13   C) 15   D) 17

21. If $(x-2)(x+3) = (x-a)(x+b)$ for all real x, then (a,b) could be | 21.

    A) $(-2,-3)$ B) $(2,-3)$ C) $(-3,2)$ D) $(-3,-2)$

22. $\dfrac{\frac{1}{x}+\frac{1}{y}}{x+y} =$ | 22.

    A) 1   B) $\frac{1}{xy}$ C) xy D) $x + y$

Go on to the next page ▐▶ **A**

23. Only _?_ different right triangles have leg-lengths $\sqrt{a}$ and $\sqrt{b}$ and hypotenuse-length $\sqrt{2003}$, where a and b are integers and $a > b > 0$.
    A) 1001   B) 1002   C) 2002   D) 2003

23.

24. When I ride my bike at the constant rate of k km every h hours, it takes me _?_ hours to ride my bike h km.

    A) $\frac{k}{h}$ B) $\frac{h}{k}$ C) $\frac{k^2}{h}$ D) $\frac{h^2}{k}$

24.

25. If $p\%$ of x is equal to 1, then $\frac{1}{p}\%$ of x is equal to

    A) $\frac{x}{10000}$ B) $\frac{x^2}{10000}$ C) $\frac{x}{100}$ D) $\frac{x^2}{100}$

25.

26. The product of both values of x for which $2003^{x^2+2x-35} = 1$ is

    A) –2   B) 2   C) –35   D) 35

26.

27. How many pairs of positive integers (a,c) satisfy $a^3+125 = c^3$?
    A) 0   B) 1   C) 2   D) 3

27.

28. If the reciprocals of 60, 65, and c are the lengths of the sides of a right triangle, and if $c > 65$, then $c =$

    A) $\sqrt{7825}$ B) $3900 \div \sqrt{7825}$
    C) 70   D) 156

28.

29. It took me a while to learn how to flip flapjacks. In fact, if $a + \frac{1}{a} = 6$, then the value of $a^2 + \frac{1}{a^2}$ is the number of attempts it took me.

    How many attempts did it take me?

    A) 34   B) 35   C) 36   D) 38

29.

30. If $3^a = 2$ and $7^b = 5$, then $9^{4a} \times 49^{2b} =$
    A) $2^4 \times 5^2$ B) $2^6 \times 5^6$ C) $2^8 \times 5^4$ D) $2^4 \times 5^8$

30.

The end of the contest  **A**

Visit our Web site at http://www.mathleague.com

Solutions on Page 121 • Answers on Page 149

2003-2004 Annual Algebra Course 1 Contest

Spring, 2004

Instructions

- **Time** You will have only *30 minutes* working time for this contest. You might be *unable* to finish all 30 questions in the time allowed.

- **Scores** Please remember that *this is a contest, not a test*—and there is no "passing" or "failing" score. Few students score as high as 24 points (80% correct). Students with half that, 12 points, *deserve commendation!*

- **Format and Point Value** This is a multiple-choice contest. Each answer is an A, B, C, or D. Write each answer in the *Answer Column* to the right of each question. A correct answer is worth 1 point. Unanswered questions get no credit. You **may** use a calculator.

1. $(2^2)(2^0)(2^0)(2^4) =$

   A) 0   B) 2^6 C) 2^8 D) 2^{2004}

   1.

2. Hairy and Beary ran home. Hairy took x minutes. Beary took 1 minute longer. The product of the number of minutes they took is

   A) $2x^2+1$ B) $2x+1$

   C) x^2+1 D) x^2+x

   2.

3. $-100 - (-10) = \underline{\ ?\ } + 10$

   A) -110 B) -100 C) -90 D) 100

   3.

4. $100 \div 10 \times 10 + 10 \times 10 =$

   A) 101   B) 110   C) 200   D) 1100

   4.

5. $(-1)^2+(-1)^0+(-1)^0+(-1)^4 =$ A) 2   B) 4   C) 6   D) 8

   5.

6. If p is prime, then p^2 has exactly $\underline{\ ?\ }$ different positive divisors.

   A) 1   B) 2   C) 3   D) 4

   6.

7. $(234+567)^2 = 234^2 + 567^2 + \underline{\ ?\ }$

   A) 0   B) $234+567$ C) 234×567 D) 468×567

   7.

8. $\dfrac{x^2+1}{x^2} =$ A) $1+\dfrac{1}{x^2}$ B) $1+x^2$ C) $x^2+\dfrac{1}{x^2}$ D) $\dfrac{1}{x^2}$

   8.

9. Al bought 12 DVDs. Ali bought 15 CDs. Each DVD cost 1.5 times as much as each CD. The ratio of Al's total cost to Ali's was

   A) 4:5   B) 5:4   C) 5:6   D) 6:5

   9.

10. Mary resisted dunking her doughnut for $b\%$ of a minutes. For how many minutes did Mary resist dunking her doughnut?

    A) ab B) $\dfrac{ab}{10}$ C) $\dfrac{ab}{100}$ D) $\dfrac{ab}{1000}$

    10.

11. $\sqrt{2^2} + \sqrt{2^4} + \sqrt{2^6} =$

    A) $2+4+8$ B) $2 \times 4 \times 8$ C) $2+4+6$ D) $2 \times 4 \times 6$

    11.

Go on to the next page ⫸ **A**

12. If $x+3$ is a factor of x^2+a, then a must equal

A) –9 B) –3 C) 3 D) 9

12.

13. If $x^2 = 5$, then $(x+1)(x-1) =$

A) –24 B) 24 C) –4 D) 4

13.

14. When $x(x[x(x+2)+2]+2)+2$ is multiplied out and like terms are combined, the result has exactly _?_ terms.

A) 4 B) 5 C) 6 D) 8

14.

15. $\dfrac{1}{x^2} + \dfrac{1}{y^2} = \dfrac{?}{x^2 y^2}$

A) 1 B) 2 C) $x^2 y^2$ D) $x^2 + y^2$

15.

16. Square S has side-length x. The sum of the numerical value of the area of S and the numerical value of the perimeter of S is

A) $x(x+4)$ B) $(x+2)(x+2)$ C) $(x+4)^2$ D) $4x^3$

16.

17. Two values of x satisfy $(x-9)^2 = 1$. These values differ by

A) 0 B) 2 C) 9 D) 18

17.

18. Which of the following is the square of a binomial?

A) x^2+x+9 B) x^2+4x+9 C) x^2+6x+9 D) x^2+9x+9

18.

19. Which of the following are the coordinates of a point that is equidistant from the coordinate axes?

A) (100,–100) B) (0,100) C) (–100,0) D) (0,–100)

19.

20. $(x^2-1)(x^2-4)(x^2-9)(x^2-16) = 0$ is satisfied by _?_ different integers.

A) 0 B) 4 C) 8 D) 16

20.

And the winning number...

21. The roots of the equation $x^2+bx+c = 0$ are 4 and 5. If the winning lottery number is $b+c$, then the winning lottery number is

A) 9 B) 11 C) 19 D) 21

21.

Go on to the next page ⟫ **A**

22. If $x = \underline{\ ?\ }$, then $x(x+1)(x+2)\times\ldots\times(x+99)(x+100) \neq 0$.

A) -98 B) -99 C) -100 D) -101

22.

23. What is the coefficient of x^1 in the complete expansion of $(x+1)^{20}$?

A) 400   B) 20   C) 19   D) 1

23.

24. $\dfrac{1}{x-\frac{1}{x}}$ is undefined for $\underline{\ ?\ }$ values of x.

A) 1   B) 2   C) 3   D) 4

24.

25. If $x+2 = y+4$, then $x^2+4x+4 =$

A) y^2+16 B) $y^2+8y+16$
C) $y^2+4y+20$ D) y^2+4y+6

25.

26. If $a, b,$ and $\sqrt{ab+b}$ are integers, then $\underline{\ ?\ }$ must also be an integer.

A) $\sqrt{b(a+1)^0}$ B) $\sqrt{b(a+1)^2}$ C) $\sqrt{b(a+1)^3}$ D) $\sqrt{b(a+1)^4}$

26.

27. Line ℓ is perpendicular to line k. If the slope of ℓ is a non-zero integer, then the slope of ℓ divided by the slope of k could equal

A) $\dfrac{1}{4}$ B) $-\dfrac{1}{4}$ C) 4   D) -4

27.

28. My phone number has 7 digits. Their product is an even perfect square. The greatest possible value of their sum is

A) 28   B) 58   C) 61   D) 63

28.

29. Our square bulletin board has area A and perimeter P. If A/P is an integer, then the length of one of the board's sides could be

A) 456   B) 567
C) 678   D) 789

29.

30. In a sequence of $2n$ positive numbers whose first term is k, each successive term is the reciprocal of the term that came before it. The sum of all $2n$ terms is

A) $\dfrac{nk^2+n}{k}$ B) $\dfrac{nk^2+n}{2k}$ C) $\dfrac{k^2+1}{kn}$ D) $\dfrac{n+k}{k^2}$

30.

The end of the contest ✍ **A**

2004-2005 Annual Algebra Course 1 Contest

Spring, 2005

Instructions

- **Time** You will have only *30 minutes* working time for this contest. You might be *unable* to finish all 30 questions in the time allowed.

- **Scores** Please remember that *this is a contest, not a test*—and there is no "passing" or "failing" score. Few students score as high as 24 points (80% correct). Students with half that, 12 points, *deserve commendation!*

- **Format and Point Value** This is a multiple-choice contest. Each answer is an A, B, C, or D. Write each answer in the *Answer Column* to the right of each question. A correct answer is worth 1 point. Unanswered questions get no credit. You **may** use a calculator.

1. $1^{2005} + 1^{2005} =$

   A) 1^{4010} B) 2^1 C) 2^{2005} D) 2^{4010}

1.

2. From n piles of 12 coconuts each, I am able to make _?_ piles of 3 coconuts each.

   A) $n+3$ B) $n+4$ C) $3n$ D) $4n$

2.

3. $x^{400} \div x^{100} =$

   A) x^{500} B) x^{300} C) x^4 D) 4

3.

4. $(-1)^1 + (-1)^2 + (-1)^3 + \ldots + (-1)^{98} + (-1)^{99} =$

   A) 1   B) 0   C) -1 D) -99

4.

5. If $x^2-y^2 = 10$, and $x+y = 10$, then $x-y =$

   A) 1   B) -1 C) 10   D) -10

5.

6. The total value of $2x$ nickels and x dimes is 60¢ when $x =$

   A) 6   B) 4   C) 3   D) 2

6.

7. The least common multiple of 2, 4, and 8 is

   A) 2   B) 8   C) 16   D) 64

7.

8. $2 = \sqrt{8} \div$ _?_

   A) 4   B) $\sqrt{6}$ C) $\sqrt{4}$ D) $\sqrt{2}$

8.

9. There are 6 more football players wearing dark helmets than wearing light ones. The ratio of dark helmets to light is 2:1. The number of light helmets is

   A) 2   B) 3   C) 6   D) 12

9.

10. The graph of _?_ is parallel to the graph of $2x+y = -3$.

    A) $2x+y = 3$ B) $2x+4y = 6$ C) $2x-y = 3$ D) $x+2y = -3$

10.

11. Of 5 consecutive integers whose average is x, the smallest is

    A) $x-2$ B) $x-3$ C) $x-4$ D) $x-5$

11.

Go on to the next page ⠿➡ **A**

12. Of 5 consecutive *even* integers whose average is x, the smallest is

    A) $x-2$ B) $x-3$ C) $x-4$ D) $x-5$

    12.

13. The greatest common factor of 2^{2004} and 2^{2005} is

    A) 1   B) 2   C) 2^{2004} D) 2^{2005}

    13.

14. I ran away with a big prize when I was the 7th caller to know that the slope of every horizontal line is

    A) 0   B) 1   C) –1   D) nonexistent

    14.

15. If 10% of a is b, then $a =$

    A) $0.1b$ B) b C) $9b$ D) $10b$

    15.

16. For which of the following is n^n the square of an integer?

    A) $n = 3$ B) $n = 5$ C) $n = 6$ D) $n = 7$

    16.

17. If $k = \underline{\ ?\ }$, then the two roots of $x^2+4x+k = 0$ are equal.

    A) 1   B) 2   C) 3   D) 4

    17.

18. Jesse has worn the same hat for d years. If he wears it for 12 more years, he will have worn this hat for d^2 years. For how many years has Jesse worn this hat?

    A) 4   B) 6   C) 8   D) 12

    18.

19. $|x| + |-x| =$

    A) 0   B) $|x|$ C) $|-x|$ D) $2|x|$

    19.

20. Circle C's center is $(0,0)$, and the length of C's radius is 5. Which of the following are the coordinates of a point on C?

    A) $(0,5)$ B) $(-5,-5)$ C) $(-10,0)$ D) $(5,5)$

    20.

21. For primes a and b, if $a > b$, then ab has $\underline{\ ?\ }$ unequal positive factors.

    A) 4   B) 3   C) 2   D) 1

    21.

22. The product of $\underline{\ ?\ }$ and x^{100} has the same value as $(-x)^{100}$.

    A) 100   B) 1   C) –1   D) –100

    22.

Go on to the next page ⟾ **A**

23. $\sqrt{16^{16}}$ =

A) 16^8 B) 16^4 C) 4^8 D) 4^4

24. If a circle's area is 3600π, then its circumference is

A) 60   B) 60π C) 120   D) 120π

25. The cheapest way to move is by mail, so each time I move, I mail myself to my new home. I've done this as many times as the number of different *integers* that satisfy $(n^2-1)(n^2-2)(n^2-3) = 0$. How many times did I move by mail?

A) 1   B) 2   C) 3   D) 6

26. $\frac{1}{x} + \frac{1}{y} + \frac{1}{xy} = \frac{?}{xy}$

A) 2   B) 3   C) $x+y+1$ D) $x+y$

27. If the sum of the squares of two numbers is equal to the square of their sum, then the product of these two numbers must be

A) 0   B) 1   C) 4   D) 16

28. $[(x+1)^2+(x+2)^2+(x+3)^2] - [(x^2+1^2)+(x^2+2^2)+(x^2+3^2)]$ =

A) 0   B) $6x$ C) $9x$ D) $12x$

29. The number of fish that swam with me is the *sum of the digits* of the largest integer x which satisfies $\frac{x}{x+1} < \frac{2004}{2005}$. How many fish swam with me?

A) 4   B) 5   C) 6   D) 7

30. For how many different integral values of b are both roots of $x^2+bx-16 = 0$ integers?

A) 3   B) 4   C) 5   D) 6

The end of the contest ✍ **A**

Solutions on Page 129 • Answers on Page 151

2005-2006 Annual Algebra Course 1 Contest

Spring, 2006

Instructions

- **Time** You will have only *30 minutes* working time for this contest. You might be *unable* to finish all 30 questions in the time allowed.

- **Scores** Please remember that *this is a contest, not a test*—and there is no "passing" or "failing" score. Few students score as high as 24 points (80% correct). Students with half that, 12 points, *deserve commendation!*

- **Format and Point Value** This is a multiple-choice contest. Each answer is an A, B, C, or D. Write each answer in the *Answer Column* to the right of each question. A correct answer is worth 1 point. Unanswered questions get no credit. You **may** use a calculator.

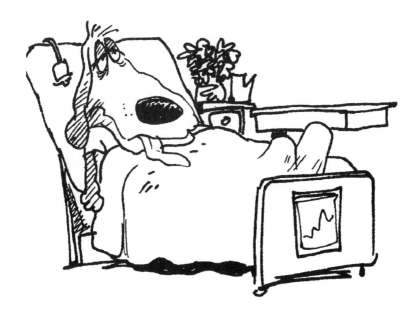

1. $(2+0+0+6)^{(2\times0\times0\times6)} =$

1.

A) 1   B) 8   C) 0   D) 8^8

2. $(-2)(-4)(-6)(-8)(-10) = (1)(2)(3)(4)(5)(\underline{\ ?\ })$

2.

A) 2   B) -2   C) 32   D) -32

3. If $x+1$ scoops of ice cream cost \$3, then $(x+1)+(2x+2)$ scoops of ice cream cost

3.

A) \$18   B) \$15
C) \$12   D) \$9

4. If $\dfrac{x^2-4}{x+2} = 8$, then $x-2 =$

4.

A) 10   B) 8   C) 6   D) 4

5. $(10x)^{100} = (10x^{100})(\underline{\ ?\ })$

5.

A) 1   B) 10   C) 10^{99} D) 10^{100}

6. One value of x for which $x^2-x < 0$ is

6.

A) 2   B) 1   C) 0.5   D) -0.5

7. How many different positive integers satisfy $\dfrac{x}{3} < 3$?

7.

A) 9   B) 8   C) 6   D) 3

8. Rectangle R has area 48 and integral side-lengths. The ratio of the length of R's longer side to that of its shorter side *cannot* be

8.

A) $3:1$ B) $6:1$ C) $12:1$ D) $48:1$

9. In my soccer league, the ratio of the number of teams that wear red jerseys to the number of teams that wear blue jerseys is 7:13. What percent of the teams in my league wear red jerseys?

9.

A) 70%   B) 49%   C) 35%   D) 20%

10. The least common multiple of x^2 and $2x$ is

10.

A) $2x$ B) $2x^2$ C) $2x^3$ D) $2x^4$

11. $x^{18}+2x^{17}+x^{16} = (\underline{\ ?\ })(x+1)^2$

11.

A) x^4 B) x^8 C) x^{12} D) x^{16}

Go on to the next page **A**

12. When I was as sick as a dog, I spent $|2x|+|-x|$ days in the hospital. I was in the hospital a total of ? days.
   A) $3x$ B) x
   C) $|x|$ D) $3|x|$

12.

13. If $x = 1$ billion, which of the following has the greatest value?
   A) $\sqrt{x^{100}}$ B) x^{20} C) $x^{10}\sqrt{x^{10}}$ D) $x^2\sqrt{x^{50}}$

13.

14. The product of all real values of x that satisfy $x^2-2006 = 0$ is
   A) 2006   B) 5002   C) $2\sqrt{2006}$ D) -2006

14.

15. A square whose area is $(x+1)^4$ has a perimeter of
   A) $4(x+1)^2$ B) $(x+1)^2$ C) $4(x+1)$ D) $(4x+1)$

15.

16. $\dfrac{w^2w^4w^6\times...\times w^{48}w^{50}}{w^1w^3w^5\times...\times w^{47}w^{49}} =$
   A) w^{24} B) w^{25} C) w^{49} D) w^{50}

16.

17. The number of fish in my fish bowl equals the number of positive integers less than 100 that are both perfect squares and perfect cubes. How many fish are in my fish bowl?
   A) 1   B) 2   C) 3   D) 64

17.

18. If each of three parallel lines has an integral slope, then the product of their slopes *cannot* be
   A) -1 B) 0   C) 1   D) 2

18.

19. If $y = 2x+5$ and $3y = ax+b$ have the same graph, then $a+b =$
   A) 7   B) 13   C) 21   D) 30

19.

20. My age in years is a two-digit number. Reversing the digits of my age results in my age 18 years ago. What is the difference between the digits of my age?
   A) 1   B) 2   C) 3   D) 4

20.

21. If $\sqrt{M\times A\times T\times H} = M\times A\times T$, then the value of H must be
   A) $M\times A\times T$ B) $\sqrt{M\times A\times T}$ C) $M^2\times A^2\times T^2$ D) 1

21.

Go on to the next page ⏵ **A**

22. If the total value of d dimes and n nickels equals the value of $(n-d)$ quarters, then $d{:}n =$

A) 4:7   B) 7:4   C) 1:2   D) 2:1

22.

23. From the 99 integers $\{1, \ldots, 99\}$, choose n different integers. If the product of these n integers is 100, the greatest possible value of n is

A) 2   B) 3   C) 4   D) 5

23.

24. $\dfrac{1}{x+\dfrac{2005}{x+2006}}$ is undefined for _?_ values of x.

A) 1   B) 2   C) 3   D) 4

24.

25. What is the least positive integer whose square is divisible by 4^{144}?

A) 4^{12} B) 4^{72} C) 4^{144} D) 4^{288}

25.

26. $\dfrac{x^2+\maltese+1}{x+y}$ is equal to $x-y + \dfrac{1}{x+y}$ whenever $\maltese =$

A) $-y^2$ B) xy C) y^2 D) $-xy$

26.

27. If $x^2-a^2 = 0$ has two real roots, then _?_ also has two real roots.

A) $x-a = 0$ B) $x+a = 0$ C) $x^2+a^2 = 0$ D) $x^4-a^4 = 0$

27.

28. If (a, b) is in quadrant II, then $(-a,-b)$ is in quadrant

A) I   B) II   C) III   D) IV

28.

29. In the sequence 4, 8, 64, . . . , each term after the first is the product of all the positive integer factors of the previous term. What is the fourth term of this sequence?

A) 2^{36} B) 2^{21} C) 2^{12} D) 2^{11}

29.

30. Any x which satisfies _?_ also satisfies $1-|x+1| < 0$.

A) $x < -2$ B) $x > -1$ C) $x < 0$ D) $x < 1$

30.

The end of the contest ✍ **A**

Visit our Web site at http://www.mathleague.com

Solutions on Page 133 • Answers on Page 152

Detailed Solutions

●●●●●●●●●●●●●●●●●

2001-2002 through 2005-2006

7th Grade Solutions

2001-2002 through 2005-2006

Information & Solutions

Tuesday, February 19 or 26, 2002

Contest Information

7

- **Solutions** Turn the page for detailed contest solutions (written in the question boxes) and letter answers (written in the *Answers* column to the right of each question).

- **Scores** Please remember that *this is a contest, not a test*—and there is no "passing" or "failing" score. Few students score as high as 30 points (75% correct). Students with half that, 15 points, *deserve commendation!*

- **Answers & Rating Scale** Turn to page 138 for the letter answers to each question and the rating scale for this contest.

1. $50 + 100 + 150 + 200 = 500 = 4 \times 125$.
   A) 75　　　　B) 100　　　　C) 125　　　　D) 133

1. C

2. I began with 68 dimes, worth $6.80. Altogether, the ten piles could have 10, 20, 30, 40, 50, or 60 dimes. Subtracting each from 68 dimes, I'd have 58, 48, 38, 28, 18, or 8 dimes left over, respectively.
   A) 12　　　　B) 24　　　　C) 36　　　　D) 48

2. D

3. Sum = 9.879. Thousandths' digit is 9, so round the 7 to 8 to get 9.88.
   A) 1.89　　B) 9.879　　C) 9.88　　D) 18.87

3. C

4. 12 hrs before midnight is noon, and 5 hrs before noon is 7 A.M.
   A) 5 A.M.　　　B) 7 A.M.
   C) 5 P.M.　　　D) 7 P.M.

4. B

5. $4^2+2^2 = 16+4 = 20 = 25-5 = 5^2-5$.
   A) 1　　B) 2　　C) 4　　D) 5

5. D

6. $A = 10^{10}$, $B = 10^3$, $C = 10^2$, and $D = 10^1$, so choice A is the largest.
   A) 10^{10}　　　B) 10×100　　　C) 10×10　　　D) 10×1^{10}

6. A

7. $3^3+3^2+3^1 = 27+9+3 = 39 = 3 \times 13$. A) 3×5 B) 3×6 C) 3×11 D) 3×13

7. D

8. A diagonal connects opposite corners, so you get 2 triangles.
   A) triangles　　B) rhombuses　C) squares　　D) rectangles

8. A

9. $\frac{1}{2} \times 1$ day $= \frac{1}{2} \times (\frac{1}{7} \times 1$ week$)$.　　　A) $\frac{1}{7}$　B) $\frac{2}{7}$　C) $\frac{1}{14}$　D) $\frac{1}{28}$

9. C

10. Ten million ÷ 100 thousand $= 10\,000\,000 \div 100\,000 = 100$.
    A) 10　　　　B) 100　　　　C) 1000　　　　D) 10 000

10. B

11. One ream has 500 sheets; 20 reams have $20 \times 500 = 10\,000$ sheets.
    A) 25 sheets　　B) 500 sheets　　C) 1000 sheets　　D) 10 000 sheets

11. D

12. The respective hundredths' digits of A, B, C, D are 8, 9, 6, 0.
    A) 79.68　　　　B) 86.79　　　　C) 97.86　　　　D) 678.9

12. B

13. $111 \times 1000 = 111\,000$ has 6 digits, and 111×999 is just 111 less.
    A) 6　　B) 5　　C) 4　　D) 3

13. A

14. 40 is 30 more than 10, which is 40 less than 50.
    A) 70　　B) 50　　C) 30　　D) 10

14. B

15. The 4 math books and 1 cookbook were non-fiction, so 5 of the 8 books, or 62.5% of the books, were non-fiction.
    A) 37.5%　　　　B) 50%
    C) 60%　　　　D) 62.5%

15. D

Go on to the next page ⫸ **7**

16. Since the square root of the perimeter of the square is 6, the perimeter is $6^2 = 36$, a side is $36 \div 4 = 9$, and the area is $9^2 = 81$. A) 36 B) 64 C) 81 D) 144	16. C
17. When I sell 33 flags at 3 for \$1 and the last 2 flags for 75¢, I charge \$11.75. When I sell 35 flags in any other way, I charge more.  A) \$11.75 B) \$11.90 C) \$12.00 D) \$14.00	17. A
18. $2 \times 500 + 2 \times 501 = 1000 + 1002 = 2002 = 2 \times 1001 = 2 \times (500 + 501)$. A) $2 + (500 \times 501)$ B) $2 \times (500 + 501)$ C) $(2 + 2) \times (500 + 501)$ D) $(2 \times 2) + (500 \times 501)$	18. B
19. The reciprocal of a product is the product of all the reciprocals. A) $\frac{3}{8} \times \frac{13}{18}$ B) $\frac{3}{13} \times \frac{8}{18}$ C) $\frac{8}{3} \times \frac{18}{13}$ D) $\frac{3}{8} \times \frac{18}{13}$	19. D
20. Side-length = perimeter ÷ (# of sides); for a $\triangle$, side-length = $36 \div 3$. A) a triangle B) a square C) a rhombus D) a hexagon	20. A
21. The even whole number factors of 36 are 2, 4, 6, 12, 18, and 36. A) 5 B) 6 C) 7 D) 8	21. B
22. To inc the avg of 20 #s by 2, increase each by 2, sum by $20 \times 2 = 40$. A) 2 B) 10 C) 22 D) 40	22. D
23. $\frac{2+3+4}{8+9+10} = \frac{9}{27} = \frac{1}{3} = \frac{8}{24} = \frac{8}{(8-1)+(9-1)+(10-1)}$.  A) 4 B) 6 C) 8 D) 9	23. C
24. If 5 scoops weigh 2 kg, then 1 scoop weighs $2/5$ kg, and 13 scoops weigh $13 \times 2/5 = 26/5$ kg. A) $\frac{13}{10}$ kg B) 5 kg C) $\frac{26}{5}$ kg D) 7 kg	24. C
25. Since $\sqrt{4} + \sqrt{16} = 6$, choice B is correct. A) $\sqrt{12} \approx 3.5$ B) $\sqrt{20} \approx 4.5$ C) $\sqrt{64} = 8$ D) $\sqrt{100} = 10$	25. B
26. $\frac{1}{4}$ of $\frac{1}{4}\% = \left(\frac{1}{4} \times \frac{1}{4}\right)\%$. A) $\frac{1}{16}\%$ B) $\frac{1}{8}\%$ C) $\frac{1}{4}\%$ D) 1%	26. A
27. Area $= \pi r^2 = \pi$ cm^2; so $r^2 = 1$ cm^2, $r = 1$ cm, and $d = 2 \times r = 2$ cm. A) π cm B) 2π cm C) 1 cm D) 2 cm	27. D
28. The greatest common factor of $\sqrt{16} = 4$ and $\sqrt{64} = 8$ is 4. A) 16 B) 8 C) 4 D) 2	28. C
29. Each congruent triangle has 1/4 the area of the square. The area of the square is $6^2 = 36$, so the area of one triangle is $36 \div 4 = 9$. A) 6 B) 9 C) $9\sqrt{2}$ D) 18	29. B

Go on to the next page ⮕ **7**

30. Add 1 to each perfect square < 200 to get 2, 5, 10, 17, 26, 37, 50, 65, 82, 101, 122, 145, 170, 197. The 6 primes are 2, 5, 17, 37, 101, 197.

    A) 5   B) 6   C) 9   D) 14

30.

B

31. Triple in 18 yrs ⇒ double in half that, 9 years, Pat's current age.

    A) 9 years   B) 12 years   C) 18 years   D) 24 years

31.

C

32. Median is the average of $\frac{1}{4}$ and $\frac{1}{5} = \left(\frac{1}{4} + \frac{1}{5}\right) \div 2 = \frac{9}{20} \div 2 = \frac{9}{40}$.

    A) $\frac{1}{9}$ B) $\frac{1}{4.5}$ C) $\frac{1}{3}$ D) $\frac{9}{40}$

32.

D

33. In a poll of more than 1 million people, exactly $16\frac{2}{3}\% = 1/6$ felt run-down. The only choice that's divisible by 6 is choice C.

    A) 2   B) 4   C) 6   D) 8

33.

C

34. $\frac{35}{4}$ cm = $\frac{35}{4} \div 100$ m = $\frac{35}{400}$ m = $\frac{7}{80}$ m.

    A) $\frac{1}{25}$ B) $\frac{7}{80}$ C) $\frac{4}{35}$ D) $\frac{35}{4}$

34.

B

35. $\sqrt{\sqrt{81}} = \sqrt{9} = 3 = (\sqrt{3})^2$.

    A) $\sqrt{3}$ B) 3   C) $3\sqrt{3}$ D) 9

35.

A

36. The reciprocal of 1 is 1. The least possible such sum is $1+1 = 2$.

    A) 2.5   B) 2   C) 1   D) 0

36.

B

37. The sum of any 3 consecutive integers is divisible by 3. Only choice B is divisible by 3. The side-lengths would be 666, 667, 668.

    A) 2000   B) 2001   C) 2002   D) 2003

37.

B

38. $\left(\frac{1}{2} \times \frac{1}{3}\right) \div (2 \times 3) = \left(\frac{1}{2} \times \frac{1}{3}\right) \times \left(\frac{1}{2} \times \frac{1}{3}\right) = \left(\frac{1}{2} \times \frac{1}{3} \times \frac{1}{2}\right) \times \left(\frac{1}{3}\right) = \frac{1}{12} \times \frac{1}{3}$.

    A) $\frac{1}{12}$ B) $\frac{1}{72}$ C) 3   D) 36

38.

A

39. In 1 hour, I drive 40 km. If I want to drive 60 km in a half-hour, I must triple my speed to 120 km/hr.

    A) 60 km/hr   B) 80 km/hr
    C) 120 km/hr   D) 160 km/hr

39.

C

40. The 30 even factors are $2^a \times 3^b$, $a = 1, 2, 3, 4, 5$, while $b = 0, 1, 2, 3, 4, 5$.

    A) 5   B) 6   C) 25   D) 30

40.

D

The end of the contest ✍ **7**

Information & Solutions

Tuesday, February 18 or 25, 2003

Contest Information

7

- **Solutions** Turn the page for detailed contest solutions (written in the question boxes) and letter answers (written in the *Answers* column to the right of each question).

- **Scores** Please remember that *this is a contest, not a test*—and there is no "passing" or "failing" score. Few students score as high as 30 points (75% correct). Students with half that, 15 points, *deserve commendation!*

- **Answers & Rating Scale** Turn to page 139 for the letter answers to each question and the rating scale for this contest.

1. $44444+88888 = 44444+22222+66666 = 66666+66666 = 66666\times2.$
   A) 2   B) 6   C) 20   D) 66 666

   1. A

2. The tens' digit of 642 is 4; this is the double of 2.
   A) 1   B) 2   C) 3   D) 4

   2. B

3. B is divisible by 5, C is even, and D is divisible by 3.
   A) $243+40 = 283$ B) $497+28 = 525$ C) $640+42 = 682$ D) $720+81 = 801$

   3. A

4. $202+2002 = 2204 = 203+2003-2.$
   A) 1   B) 2   C) 3   D) 4

   4. B

5. Since 2 hops = 4 hip-hops, 4 hops = 8 hip-hops. Since 2 hips = 1 hop, 8 hips = 4 hops = 8 hip-hops.
   A) 2   B) 4   C) 8   D) 16

   5. C

6. $(2+4+6)^2 = 12^2 = 144 = 36\times4 = 6^2\times4 = (1+2+3)^2\times4.$
   A) $(1+2+3)^4$ B) $(1+2+3)\times2$ C) $(1+2+3)^2\times4$ D) $2^2+4^2+6^2$

   6. C

7. The last digit of 99.99 is the hundredths' digit; it's already rounded.
   A) 100.09   B) 100   C) 99.99   D) 99.1

   7. C

8. $(200\times300) + (20\times30) + (2\times3) = 60\,606 = (2\times3)\times10\,101.$
   A) 111   B) 10 101   C) 60 600   D) 60 606

   8. B

9. $33+66+99 = 33\times(1+2+3) = 11\times(3+6+9) = 22\times(3+3+3).$
   A) $1+2+3$ B) $3+6+9$ C) $3+3+3$ D) $9+9+9$

   9. D

10. $\frac{1}{3} + \left(-\frac{1}{3}\right) = 0$, so A is correct.   A) $-\frac{1}{3}$ B) -3 C) $\frac{2}{3}$ D) 3

    10. A

11. The pizza's diameter equals the side-length of the box top. The perimeter = 4 side-lengths = $4\times(2\times radius) = 4\times(2\times70)$ cm.
    A) 140 cm   B) 140π cm   C) 280 cm   D) 560 cm

    11. D

12. $5 = \frac{8}{10}\times\frac{6}{8}\times\frac{4}{6}\times\frac{2}{4}\times\underline{?} = \frac{1}{5}\times\underline{?}$, so $5 = \frac{1}{5}\times25.$
    A) 1   B) 4   C) 16   D) 25

    12. D

13. During the past 4 years, 3 years had 365 days and 1 year had 366 days (a leap year). The average is $(365+365+365+366) \div 4 = 365.25$, which is choice B.
    A) 365.00   B) 365.25   C) 365.33   D) 365.50

    13. B

14. $5 \div \frac{2}{6} = 5\times\frac{6}{2} = 5\times3.$ A) 4   B) 3   C) $\frac{3}{2}$ D) $\frac{1}{3}$

    14. B

Go on to the next page ⟱ 7

78

15. In order, the tenths' digits of the choices are 3, 0, 7, and 3.

    A) 0.3073   B) 3.073   C) 30.73   D) 307.3

    15. C

16. In the diagram at the right, the region in which they overlap is the shaded triangle.

    A) triangle   B) square   C) rhombus   D) rectangle

    16. A

17. 50 dimes ÷ 50 quarters = 1 dime ÷ 1 quarter = 10/25 = 40%.

    A) 10%   B) 30%   C) 35%   D) 40%

    17. D

18. $(999 \times 1000) - (999 \times 998) = 999 \times (1000 - 998) = 999 \times 2 = 1998.$

    A) 1000+999   B) 1000+998   C) 1000−998   D) 1000−999

    18. B

19. Since we washed cars from noon until 11:30 PM, we washed cars for 11 hrs. 30 mins. = 11 × 60 mins. + 30 mins. = 660 mins. + 30 mins.

    A) 330   B) 690   C) 1020   D) 1140

    19. B

20. $77^2 \times (77 \times 77)^2 = 77^2 \times (77^2)^2 = 77^2 \times 77^4.$

    A) 77^5 B) $77^2 \times 77^3$ C) $77^2 \times 77^4$ D) 3×77^2

    20. C

21. $3 \div 5 \div 7 = (3 \div 5) \div 7 = \frac{3}{5} \div 7 = \frac{3}{35}.$ A) $\frac{3}{35}$ B) $\frac{7}{21}$ C) $\frac{15}{7}$ D) $\frac{21}{5}$

    21. A

22. $\frac{3}{4} + \frac{1}{2} + \frac{3}{4} = \frac{8}{4} = 2.$ A) $\frac{3}{4}$ B) 1   C) $\frac{3}{2}$ D) 2

    22. D

23. $3 \div \frac{1}{6} = 3 \times 6 = 18$; its reciprocal is $\frac{1}{18} = \frac{1}{3} \times \frac{1}{6}.$

    A) $\frac{1}{3} \times \frac{1}{6}$ B) $\frac{1}{3} \times 6$ C) $3 \times \frac{1}{6}$ D) 3×6

    23. A

24. Since 72 is a multiple of 2, the largest such factor is 72.

    A) 2   B) 8   C) 36   D) 72

    24. D

25. Since \$10 = 1000¢ and \$7 = 700¢, I have 1000 ÷ 5 = 200 coins, you have 700 ÷ 10 = 70 coins, and 200−70 = 130.

    A) 30   B) 70   C) 130   D) 140

    25. C

26. If product of 3 integers is odd, each is odd & sum is odd.

    A) odd   B) even   C) positive   D) negative

    26. A

27. $\sqrt{64} - \sqrt{9} = 8 - 3 = \sqrt{25}.$ A) $\sqrt{55}$ B) $\sqrt{45}$ C) $\sqrt{25}$ D) $\sqrt{5}$

    27. C

28. Since 345−54 = 334−43, ♣ could represent subtraction.

    A) +   B) −   C) ×   D) ÷

    28. B

Go on to the next page ⏵ **7**

29. $\frac{4}{10}$ of 40 = 16 = 4×4 = 400% of 4.   A) 16   B) 40   C) 160   D) 400

29. D

30. 100 000 000 = $2^8 \times 5^8$. Like all powers of 5 ≥ 5^2, 5^8 ends in "**25**."
    A) 0   B) 2   C) 4   D) 6

30. B

31. Try 1+2+3+4+5+6+7+8+9 = 45; it's not divisible by 6.
    A) 1   B) 3   C) 6   D) 9

31. C

32. He'll need 4 corner tiles, 10 tiles for each shorter
    edge, and 14 more tiles for each longer edge.
    He'll need 4+10+10+14+14 = 52 tiles.
    A) 52   B) 56   C) 58   D) 60

32. A

33. 0.4^2 = 0.16 < 0.4.   A) 0.2^2 B) 0.2^3 C) 0.4   D) 0.4^4

33. C

34. The only such triangle has sides of length 2, 3, and 3.
    A) isosceles   B) right   C) obtuse   D) equilateral

34. A

35. Look for a pattern: $(1/10)^1$ = 0.1 has no 0; $(1/10)^2$ = 1/100 = 0.01
    has one 0; $(1/10)^3$ = 0.001 has two 0s. Similarly, $(0.1)^{100}$ has 99 0s.
    A) 98   B) 99   C) 100   D) 101

35. B

36. Lance sells 60 bikes each month. Since 1/12 of 60 = 5 =
    1/3 of the racing bikes he sold, Lance sells 3×5 = 15
    racing bikes each month.
    A) 20   B) 15   C) 12   D) 5

36. B

37. As shown, a circle can cross each side of a square twice.
    A) 2   B) 4   C) 6   D) 8

37. D

38. Possible distributions for (Ali,Bob,Carl):
    are: (3,0,0), (0,3,0), (0,0,3),
    (2,1,0), (2,0,1), (1,2,0), (1,0,2), (0,2,1), (0,1,2),
    and (1,1,1), This shows that I can
    distribute 3 pizza slices in 10 ways.
    A) 8   B) 9   C) 10   D) 12

38. C

39. 4,8,...,96 = 24 #s. 9,18,...,99 = 11 #s. 25,50,75 = 3 #s. 49,98 = 2#s.
    We counted 36 & 72 twice each, so total = 24+11+3+2−2 = 38.
    A) 36   B) 38   C) 40   D) 44

39. B

40. The hour hand makes 2, the minute hand makes 24, and the
    second hand makes 60×24 = 1440 revolutions.
    A) 72   B) 733   C) 1466   D) 10 104

40. C

The end of the contest **7**

Visit our Web site at http://www.mathleague.com

Information & Solutions

Tuesday, February 17 or 24, 2004

7

Contest Information

- **Solutions** Turn the page for detailed contest solutions (written in the question boxes) and letter answers (written in the *Answers* column to the right of each question).

- **Scores** Please remember that *this is a contest, not a test*—and there is no "passing" or "failing" score. Few students score as high as 30 points (75% correct). Students with half that, 15 points, *deserve commendation!*

- **Answers & Rating Scale** Turn to page 140 for the letter answers to each question and the rating scale for this contest.

1. $(10 + 10) \times (10 - 10) = (10 + 10) \times 0 = 0.$
   A) 0   B) 20   C) 190   D) 990

   1. A

2. Remainders for 1900, 190, and 19 are 0, 0, and 4; and $0+0+4 = 4.$
   A) 1   B) 2   C) 3   D) 4

   2. D

3. $2 + (2 \times 2) + 2 = 2 + (4) + 2 = 8 = 4 + 4 = 2^2 + 2^2.$
   A) $(2 + 2)^2$ B) $(2 \times 2)^2$ C) $2^2 \times 2^2$ D) $2^2 + 2^2$

   3. D

4. Smallest difference is $0.90 - 0.89 = 0.01$, so choice C is closest.
   A) $0.9 - 0.8 = 0.1$ B) $0.9 - 0.85 = 0.05$ C) $0.9 - 0.89 = 0.01$ D) $0.99 - 0.9 = 0.09$

   4. C

5. 30 minutes before 5 P.M. = 4:30 P.M. = 15 minutes after 4:15 P.M.
   A) 5:15   B) 4:45   C) 4:30   D) 4:15

   5. D

6. I won 50% of my tosses, so I won as many tosses as I lost. If I lost 18 times, I also won 18 times.
   A) 36   B) 27
   C) 18   D) 9

   6. C

7. $1000\,\text{m} + 10\,\text{m} + 1\,\text{m} = 1011\,\text{m}.$
   A) 111 m   B) 1010 m   C) 1011 m   D) 1110 m

   7. C

8. $4 + \dfrac{3}{2} = 4 + 1\dfrac{1}{2} = \dfrac{1}{2} + 5.$ A) $4\dfrac{1}{2}$ B) 5   C) $5\dfrac{1}{2}$ D) 6

   8. B

9. The multiples are $4 \times 1, 4 \times 2, \ldots, 4 \times 24$. There are 24 multiples.
   A) 22   B) 24   C) 25   D) 26

   9. B

10. The total increase is $64 \times 2 = 128.$
    A) 2   B) 32   C) 64   D) 128

    10. D

11. Since $0.25 = 1/4$, multiplying by 0.25 is the same as dividing by 4.
    A) 4   B) 400   C) 2.5   D) 25

    11. A

12. The average of 1000 and 2000 is 1500. Then, $2000 - 1500 = 500.$
    A) 50   B) 500   C) 1000   D) 1500

    12. B

13. The volume of a rectangular solid is length $\times$ width $\times$ height. Volume = $3 \times 4 \times 2 = 24.$
    A) 99   B) 24   C) 18   D) 9

    13. B

14. Since 4 of the 20 volunteers are supervisors, we know that $4/20 = 20/100 = 20\%$ of the volunteers are supervisors.
    A) 20%   B) 25%
    C) 75%   D) 80%

    14. A

Go on to the next page ⫸ **7**

15. 1 hr = 3600 secs; $\frac{1}{100}$ hr = $\frac{3600}{100}$ secs A) $\frac{1}{100}$ B) $\frac{36}{60}$ C) $\frac{1}{36}$ D) $\frac{1}{3600}$	15. A
16. $999 \times (183 - 182) = 999$. A) 1 B) 182 C) 183 D) 999	16. D
17. If my sister has 3 brothers and 2 sisters, there are 3 male and 3 female siblings. Each of my brothers has 2 brothers and 3 sisters. A) 2, 2 B) 2, 3 C) 3, 2 D) 3, 3	17. B
18. $\frac{9}{4} \times \frac{9}{4} \times \frac{9}{4} = \frac{729}{64}$. A) $\frac{8}{64}$ B) $\frac{27}{64}$ C) $8\frac{1}{64}$ D) $\frac{729}{64}$	18. D
19. The balls are numbered 1, 2, 3, 4, 5, 6, 7, 8, and 9. Since 4 of the 9 balls have even numbers, the probability that the number on the ball that I selected was even is 4/9. A) $\frac{1}{5}$ B) $\frac{1}{4}$ C) $\frac{4}{9}$ D) $\frac{5}{9}$ 	19. C
20. $\frac{1}{2} + \frac{1}{3} = \frac{5}{6} = 1 \div \frac{6}{5}$. A) 6 B) $\frac{6}{5}$ C) $\frac{5}{6}$ D) $\frac{1}{5}$	20. B
21. Try some: 1/2, 1/3, 1/4, . . . , all of which are less than 1. A) less than 1 B) more than 1 C) odd D) negative	21. A
22. $100 \times (1/10) = 10 = 1000 \times (1/100)$. A) 10 B) 100 C) 1000 D) 10 000	22. C
23. For every performer who frowns, four performers smile. So, 4 of every 5 performers smile. This means that 4/5 of the 80 *Bike Teens* smile while performing, and 4/5 of 80 is 64. A) 16 B) 20 C) 60 D) 64	23. D
24. $\left(1+2+3+4\right) - \left(\frac{1}{5} + \frac{2}{5} + \frac{3}{5} + \frac{4}{5}\right) = 10 - \frac{10}{5}$. A) 0 B) 5 C) 8 D) 10	24. C
25. In a $\triangle$, the sum of any *two* angles is < 180°, so D is impossible. A) 80° B) 90° C) 95° D) 105°	25. D
26. $\sqrt{4^2} = 4$, $\sqrt{12^2} = 12$, $\sqrt{7^2} = 7$, so ? $= 9^2$. A) 15^2 B) 9^2 C) 6^2 D) 3^2	26. B
27. Since $3 \times 29 = 87$, the sum of the primes is $3 + 29 = 32$. A) 20 B) 30 C) 32 D) 42	27. C
28. $1\% = 1/100 = 10 \times 1/1000$. A) 0.001 B) 0.01 C) 0.1 D) 1	28. A

Go on to the next page ⫸ **7**

29. $3 \times \sqrt{25} = 15 = 5 \times \sqrt{9}$. A) $\sqrt{3}$ B) $\sqrt{9}$ C) $\sqrt{15}$ D) $\sqrt{81}$ | 29. B

30. When you divide my fraction by yours, the result is 40. When you divide your fraction by mine, the result is 1/40.

    A) 0.025   B) 0.25   C) 0.40   D) 2.50 | 30. A

31. Dimensions could be 1×48, 2×24, 3×16, 4×12, or 6×8, with perimeters 98, 52, 38, 32, and 28.

    A) $28 = 2(6+8)$ B) $38 = 2(3+16)$
    C) 58 (impossible)   D) $98 = 2(1+48)$ | 31. C

32. Since I have two nickels for every dime, my nickels are worth as much as my dimes, $3.30.

    A) $1.15 B) $3.30 C) $6.60 D) $13.20 | 32. B

33. A) $\frac{27}{63} < \frac{28}{63}$ B) $\frac{54}{117} > \frac{52}{117}$ C) $\frac{72}{153} > \frac{68}{153}$ D) $\frac{18}{27} > \frac{12}{27}$ | 33. A

34. The least multiple of 2, 4, 6, 8 is 24. The multiples of 24 are 24, 48, 72, 96, 120, 144, ... The list's first perfect square is 144.

    A) 64   B) 144   C) 576   D) 2304 | 34. B

35. $4^9 = 2^{18}$ and $9^4 = 3^8$.   A) 81^3 B) 18^3 C) 7^8 D) 3^8 | 35. D

36. The greatest common factor of 200 and 600 is 200.

    A) 10   B) 10×10 C) 10×20 D) $10 \times 20 \times 30$ | 36. C

37. $\frac{9}{7} \times \frac{7}{5} \times \frac{5}{3} = 3 = \frac{3}{5} \times \frac{5}{7} \times \frac{7}{9} \times 9$. A) 27 B) 18 C) 9 D) 3 | 37. C

38. Try the choices. Use the formula: Area $= \pi r^2$. For choice A, Area $= \frac{1}{\pi} = \pi \times \left(\frac{1}{\pi}\right)^2$. Thus, a radius of the frisbee is $\frac{1}{\pi}$.

    A) $\frac{1}{\pi}$ B) $\frac{1}{2\pi}$ C) $\frac{1}{\pi^2}$ D) $\frac{1}{2\pi^2}$ | 38. A

39. $3^1, 3^2, 3^3, 3^4$ end in 3, 9, 7, 1. This now repeats in blocks of 4. Ones' digit of 2003^{2004} is 1.

    A) 9   B) 7
    C) 3   D) 1 | 39. D

40. $\left(\frac{1}{2} + \frac{199}{2}\right) + \left(\frac{3}{2} + \frac{197}{2}\right) + \left(\frac{5}{2} + \frac{195}{2}\right) + ... = 100 + 100 + 100 + ... = 100 \times 50 = 5000$.

    A) 5000   B) 10 000   C) 15 000   D) 20 000 | 40. A

The end of the contest 🖎 **7**

Visit our Web site at http://www.mathleague.com

Information & Solutions

February 15 or 22, 2005

Contest Information

7

- **Solutions** Turn the page for detailed contest solutions (written in the question boxes) and letter answers (written in the *Answers* column to the right of each question).

- **Scores** Please remember that *this is a contest, not a test*—and there is no "passing" or "failing" score. Few students score as high as 30 points (75% correct). Students with half that, 15 points, *deserve commendation!*

- **Answers & Rating Scale** Turn to page 141 for the letter answers to each question and the rating scale for this contest.

1. 84 players can split into $84 \div 6 = 14$ teams of 6 players and $84 \div 4 = 21$ teams of 4 players. There are 7 more teams of 4.
   A) 5   B) 6   C) 7   D) 14

   1.
   C

2. $(0 \times 1) + (1 \times 10) + (0 \times 0) + 1 = 0 + 10 + 0 + 1 = 11.$
   A) 0   B) 1   C) 3   D) 11

   2.
   D

3. The sum is 180°. The 3rd angle must be $180° - (20° + 40°) = 120°.$
   A) 60°   B) 80°   C) 90°   D) 120°

   3.
   D

4. $3456 \times 0.001 = 3.456$. This rounds up to 3.5.
   A) 0.3   B) 3.4   C) 3.5   D) 34.6

   4.
   C

5. Since 720 minutes = $(720 \div 60)$ hours = 12 hours, my bad hair day began at 7:20 A.M.
   A) 1:20 A.M.   B) 7:20 A.M.
   C) 12:00 P.M.   D) 7:08 P.M.

   5.
   B

6. The sum = $5 \times 500 = 2500 = 10 \times 250.$
   A) 25   B) 50   C) 250   D) 2000

   6.
   C

7. Since every number on the list is greater than the sum of its digits, all 90 numbers are greater than the sum of their digits.
   A) 88   B) 89   C) 90   D) 99

   7.
   C

8. $1^3 + 2^4 = 17 = 1^3 + 4^2.$ A) $1^4 + 3^2$ B) $1^3 + 4^2$ C) $1^2 + 4^3$ D) $1^1 + 3^4$

   8. B

9. There are 11 prime days in May: 2, 3, 5, 7, 11, 13, 17, 19, 23, 29, and 31.
   A) 10   B) 11   C) 12   D) 13

   9.
   B

10. $(\frac{2}{3} \times \frac{3}{2}) \times (\frac{4}{5} \times \frac{5}{4}) \times (\frac{6}{7} \times \frac{7}{6}) = 1 \times 1 \times 1 = 1.$ A) 1 B) 3 C) 6 D) 12

    10. A

11. Since 5 nickels = 1 quarter, 500 nickels = 100 quarters.
    A) 100   B) 250   C) 500   D) 2500

    11.
    A

12. All side-lengths are equal, so the perimeter is divisible by 4.
    A) 33   B) 44   C) 55   D) 66

    12.
    B

13. 3 of every 150 is the same as 1 of every 50. That's the same as 2 of every 100, which is 2%.
    A) 2   B) 3   C) 5   D) 50

    13.
    A

14. $\frac{33}{50}$ cannot be reduced.
    A) $\frac{9}{15}$ B) $\frac{21}{35}$ C) $\frac{24}{40}$ D) $\frac{33}{50}$

    14.
    D

15. $\sqrt{100} = \sqrt{36} + \sqrt{?} \Leftrightarrow 10 = 6 + \sqrt{?}$, so $4 = \sqrt{?} = \sqrt{16}$.
    A) 2   B) 4   C) 16   D) 64

    15.
    C

Go on to the next page �decoration➡ **7**

16.	As shown, 2 squares with a common side form a rectangle. ☐☐ A) An octagon B) A hexagon C) A rectangle D) A triangle	16. C
17.	Each of the 9 numbers in the first sum is 1 more than the number in the same position in the second sum. A) 9 B) 10 C) 90 D) 100	17. A
18.	Uncle Bookworm eats 2 books a week, or 104 a year. Aunt Bookworm eats 1 book every 2 months, or 6 a year. Uncle eats $104-6 = 98$ more books than Aunt. A) 20 B) 40 C) 80 D) 98	18. D
19.	The largest odd factor of 81 is 81. A) 3 B) 9 C) 27 D) 81	19. D
20.	$\left(\frac{2}{3}\right)^3 = \frac{2\times2\times2}{3\times3\times3} = \frac{8}{27}$. A) 2 B) $\frac{6}{9}$ C) $\frac{8}{3}$ D) $\frac{8}{27}$	20. D
21.	To seat the most students, put the students in seats 1, 3, 5, 7, 9, 11, 13, 15, 17, 19, 21, 23, and 25. That's 13 seated students. A) 11 B) 12 C) 13 D) 24	21. C
22.	The smallest multiple of 10 that's greater than $9\times9 = 81$ is 90. A) $9\times9+10$ B) 9.1×9.1 C) 9×10 D) 10×10	22. C
23.	$\frac{6}{5} - \frac{5}{6} = \frac{36}{30} - \frac{25}{30} = \frac{11}{30}$. A) $\frac{1}{5}$ B) $\frac{1}{6}$ C) $\frac{1}{30}$ D) $\frac{11}{30}$	23. D
24.	The rear wheel's diameter is 6 cm more than the front wheel's. The rear wheel's circumference is $(d+6)\times\pi$ cm, which is 6π cm more than the front wheel's. A) 3π B) 6π C) 9π D) 36π	24. B
25.	All sides of a regular polygon have equal lengths. A) square B) equilateral C) scalene D) isosceles	25. B
26.	My age could be 8 and yours could be 16. When you divide 16 by 5, the remainder is 1. A) 1 B) 2 C) 3 D) 4	26. A
27.	If a rectangle's perimeter is 30 cm, and its area is 56 cm², then the longer side's length is 8 cm, and the shorter side's length is 7 cm. A) 1 B) 5 C) 20 D) 26	27. A
28.	Try some numbers. One set that works is 12 and 13. (The sum always exceeds the difference by twice the smaller number.) A) 0 B) 6 C) 12 D) 48	28. C

Go on to the next page ⫸ **7**

29. The 1st 12 won $12 \times \$80 = \$960$. The next 20 won $20 \times \$70 = \$1400$. The 32 contestants won an average of $\$2360 \div 32 = \$73.75$. A) \$73.75 B) \$74.75 C) \$75.00 D) \$75.75	29. A
30. $4^3 \times 4^3 = 4^{3+3} = 4^6$. A) 16^9 B) 16^6 C) 4^9 D) 4^6	30. D
31. 4 such circles fit inside a square of side-length 4. A) 1 B) 4 C) 5 D) 16	31. B
32. Just as $1 - 0.9 = 0.1$, $0.1\% = 1.0\% - 0.9\%$. A) 0.009% B) 0.09% C) 0.9% D) 10%	32. C
33. Change each answer choice to months. Since 6 years = 72 months, and 5 years ago I was 1 year old, choice A is correct. A) 6 B) 7 C) 8 D) 12	33. A
34. $\sqrt{81 \times 81 \times 81 \times 81} = \sqrt{81^4} = 81^2$, so $\sqrt{\sqrt{81 \times 81 \times 81 \times 81}} = \sqrt{81^2} = 81$. A) 3 B) 9 C) 27 D) 81	34. D
35. If a product is even, *at least* 1 factor must be even. A) 2005 B) 2004 C) 1 D) 0	35. B
36. 1/2 is one-fourth of 2, its reciprocal, so choice A is correct. A) $\frac{1}{2}$ B) $\frac{1}{4}$ C) 2 D) 4	36. A
37. $21 = 3 \times 7$; $51 = 3 \times 17$; $81 = 3 \times 27$; $91 = 7 \times 13$. Other 5 are prime. A) 4 B) 5 C) 6 D) 7	37. B
38. $(301-1) + (302-2) + \ldots + (325-25) = (300) \times 25 = 7500$. A) 25 B) 2500 C) 5000 D) 7500	38. D
39. Angle at 4:30 is 45°. Each min., the min. hand moves 6°, hr. hand moves 0.5°, so the angle increases 5.5°. The 8-min. increase is 44°, so the angle at 4:38 is only 89°. A) 4:36 B) 4:37 C) 4:38 D) 4:39	39. D
40. If $H+K+L+N = 2005$, then H is less than $2005 \div 4 = 501.25$. If $H = 498$, $H+K+L+N = 498+501+502+504 = 2005$. Since M and N are the middle of the alphabet, the average of all 26 letters is $(503+504) \div 2 = 503.5$. A) 491 B) 498 C) 503.5 D) 505.5	40. C

The end of the contest ✍ **7**

Information & Solutions

February 21 or 28, 2006

Contest Information

7

- **Solutions** Turn the page for detailed contest solutions (written in the question boxes) and letter answers (written in the *Answers* column to the right of each question).

- **Scores** Please remember that *this is a contest, not a test*—and there is no "passing" or "failing" score. Few students score as high as 30 points (75% correct). Students with half that, 15 points, *deserve commendation!*

- **Answers & Rating Scale** Turn to page 142 for the letter answers to each question and the rating scale for this contest.

1. $24242 + 42424 = 66666 = 22222 \times 3$. A) 2 B) 3 C) 4 D) 6	1. B
2. In a regular year, March 1 to February 1 is $365-28 = 337$ days. In a leap year, March 1 to February 1 is $366-29 = 337$ days. Either way, the pot of gold weighs 337 kg. A) 335 B) 336 C) 337 D) 338	2. C
3. Try examples: $3-1 = 2$; $5-3 = 2$. A) 0 B) 1 C) 2 D) 3	3. C
4. $(18+19+20+21+22) \div 5 = 100 \div 5 = 20$. A) 19 B) 20 C) 20.5 D) 21	4. B
5. $(64 \div 8) \times 4 \times 2 = 8 \times 4 \times 2 = 64$. A) 1 B) 4 C) 16 D) 64	5. D
6. 10×500 cm $= 10 \times 5$ m $= 5 \times 10$ m. A) 5000 B) 1000 C) 100 D) 10	6. D
7. Twice my age $= 120$ months $= 10$ years. My age, in years, is 5. A) 5 B) 10 C) 12 D) 60	7. A
8. Perimeter $\div 4 =$ side-length, which must be even; but $12 \div 4 = 3$. A) 12 B) 16 C) 24 D) 32	8. A
9. $(100+99+98)-(99+98+97) = 100+(99-99)+(98-98)-97 = 3$. A) 1 B) 3 C) 4 D) 97	9. B
10. We need $(64 \times 2) = 128$ slices, so we need $128 \div 8 = 16$ pizzas. A) 32 B) 16 C) 8 D) 4	10. B
11. $3^2-2^2-1^2 = 9-4-1 = 5-1 = 4$. A) 0 B) 1 C) 3 D) 4	11. D
12. If 1 Red River beaver eats as much as 6 White River beavers, and 6 White River beavers eat as much as 8 Green River beavers, then 5 Red River beavers eat as much as 5×8 Green River beavers. A) 20 B) 30 C) 40 D) 60	12. C
13. $1 \times 10^2 = 100$, $8 \times 10^1 = 80$, $10 \times 8^1 = 80$, and $18 \times 1^{10} = 18$. A) 1×10^2 B) 8×10^1 C) 10×8^1 D) 18×1^{10}	13. A
14. 1 tenth $-$ 1 hundredth $= 0.10 - 0.01 = 0.09$. A) 9.90 B) 0.99 C) 0.90 D) 0.09	14. D
15. 2 halves $=$ 3 thirds. Tripling both sides, 6 halves $=$ 9 thirds. A) 3 B) 4 C) 9 D) 12	15. C

16. $(20 \times 16 \times 12 \times 8) \div (5 \times 4 \times 3 \times 2) = 4 \times 4 \times 4 \times 4$; the remainder is 0.
    A) 0   B) 1   C) 2   D) 4

16.
A

17. Since $6^4 = (3 \times 2)^4$, $3 \times 3 \times 3 \times 3 = 9^2$ is the largest odd factor of 6^4.
    A) 3   B) 3^3 C) 9^2 D) 9^4

17.
C

18. The greatest distance is the length of a diameter $= 2 \times 2 = 4$.
    A) 1   B) 2   C) 4   D) 4π

18.
D

19. The quotient $\frac{1}{2} \div \frac{3}{4} = \frac{1}{2} \times \frac{4}{3} = \frac{2}{3} = 2 \div 3$.
    A) $\frac{3}{4}$ B) $\frac{4}{3}$ C) 3   D) 4

19.
C

20. (# nickels) in \$40 $= 2 \times$ (# dimes) in \$40 $= 4 \times$ (# dimes) in \$20.
    A) \$10   B) \$20   C) \$80   D) \$160

20.
B

21. Since $\frac{1}{2} + \frac{1}{3} = \frac{5}{6}$, its reciprocal is $\frac{6}{5}$, and $\frac{1}{5} \times \frac{6}{5} = \frac{6}{25}$.
    A) $\frac{6}{25}$ B) $\frac{6}{5}$ C) $\frac{1}{6}$ D) 1

21.
A

22. Since $\frac{1}{3} \times \frac{1}{3} = \frac{1}{9}$ of my pockets are
    empty pockets that have a hole, then $\frac{8}{9}$
    are *not* empty pockets that have a hole.
    A) $\frac{1}{3}$ B) $\frac{5}{9}$ C) $\frac{2}{3}$ D) $\frac{8}{9}$

22.
D

23. 1% of 1 $= 0.01 = $ 10% of 0.10.
    A) 10   B) 1   C) 0.10   D) 0.01

23.
C

24. The average of 0, 1, 2, . . . 12, 13, and 14 is 7. Their product is 0.
    A) 0   B) 7   C) 105   D) 5040

24.
A

25. $\sqrt{36 + 64} = \sqrt{100} = 10 = 2 \times 5 = \sqrt{4} \times \sqrt{25}$.
    A) 16   B) 25   C) 36   D) 49

25.
B

26. Since the sum of the lengths of the 2 smaller sides must *exceed*
    the length of the longest side, the longest side is at most 11.
    A) 11   B) 13   C) 16   D) 22

26.
A

27. $21 + 42 + 63 + 84 + 105 + 126 = 21 \times (1 + 2 + 3 + 4 + 5 + 6) = 21 \times 21$.
    A) 6   B) 7   C) 21   D) 42

27.
C

28. In 7 days, this truck carries $7 \times 20 =$
    140 loads. This is 140/350 $=$
    2/5 or 40% of a 350-load job.
    A) 42%   B) 40%   C) 30%   D) 6%

28.
B

29. $\frac{1+2+3}{2+4+6} + \frac{4+8+12}{1+2+3} = \frac{1}{2} + 4 = \frac{9}{2}$.
    A) 2   B) $\frac{8}{3}$ C) 4   D) $\frac{9}{2}$

29.
D

Go on to the next page ⫸ **7**

30. Any 2 such diameters share the center, so they can't be parallel. A) be perpendicular B) be parallel C) be equal in length D) have a point in common	30. B
31. $999^2 = \sqrt{999 \times 999 \times 999 \times 999} = \sqrt{999} \times \sqrt{999^3}$. A) 999 B) 999^2 C) 999^3 D) 999^4	31. C
32. The largest 3-digit prime number is 997. Since the only prime digit in 997 is 7, the answer is D. A) 1 B) 3 C) 5 D) 7	32. D
33. All powers of $5 \geq 5^2$ end in "25." A) 0 B) 2 C) 4 D) 5	33. B
34. The perfect-square multiples of 36 that are between 1×36 and 36×36 are 4×36, 9×36, 16×36, and 25×36. A) 0 B) 4 C) 9 D) 16	34. B
35. $\frac{5}{3} \div \frac{3}{5} = \frac{5}{3} \times \frac{5}{3} = \frac{25}{9}$, and $\frac{25}{9} \div \frac{3}{5} = \frac{25}{9} \times \frac{5}{3} = \frac{125}{27}$. A) $\frac{2}{5}$ B) $\frac{5}{3}$ C) $\frac{50}{18}$ D) $\frac{125}{27}$	35. D
36. $(1 \times 100) \times (2 \times 50) \times (4 \times 25) \times (5 \times 20) \times 10 \div 100 = 10^9 \div 10^2 = 10^7$. A) 1 B) 100 C) 100^4 D) 10^7	36. D
37. If $a \triangle b \triangle c = a \times c + b \times c$, then $7 \triangle 8 \triangle 9 = 7 \times 9 + 8 \times 9 = 135$. A) 128 B) 135 C) 272 D) 639	37. B
38. $1 + \dfrac{2}{3 + \frac{4}{5}} = 1 + \dfrac{2}{\frac{19}{5}} = 1 + (2 \div \frac{19}{5}) = 1 + 2 \times \frac{5}{19} = 1 + \frac{10}{19} = 1\frac{10}{19}$. A) $1\frac{10}{19}$ B) $1\frac{10}{12}$ C) $2\frac{3}{7}$ D) $8\frac{2}{5}$	38. A
39. Speedy Rabbit's average speed was (800 m)÷5 min. = 160 m/min. To finish in 4 minutes, he would have to increase his average speed to 200 m/min., a 25% increase. A) 20% B) 25% C) 30% D) 40%	39. B
40. Each time 2 rabbits drop out, one comes back in. This happens 13 times. Each time, the net loss is 1 rabbit. The number of rabbits left in the end is $50 - 13 = 37$. A) 20 B) 24 C) 37 D) 39	40. C

The end of the contest ✍️ **7**

Visit our web site at http://www.mathleague.com

8th Grade Solutions

2001-2002 through 2005-2006

Information & Solutions

Tuesday, February 19 or 26, 2002

Contest Information

8

- **Solutions** Turn the page for detailed contest solutions (written in the question boxes) and letter answers (written in the *Answers* column to the right of each question).

- **Scores** Please remember that *this is a contest, not a test*—and there is no "passing" or "failing" score. Few students score as high as 30 points (75% correct). Students with half that, 15 points, *deserve commendation!*

- **Answers & Rating Scale** Turn to page 143 for the letter answers to each question and the rating scale for this contest.

1. Add 100 to each # on the rt to get #s on the left. Total added = 300. A) 100 B) 200 C) 300 D) 600	1. C
2. My test grade was a product of two consecutive integers. Since 56 = 7×8, choice D is correct. A) 45 B) 48 C) 54 D) 56	2. D
3. Rewrite all #s with 4 places; B is greatest. A) 0.0110 B) 0.0111 C) 0.0101 D) 0.0100	3. B
4. (One-tenth of ten) dollars = $1 = 100 pennies. A) 1 B) 10 C) 100 D) 1000	4. C
5. 125 days of rain per yr ⇒ it rains either (125/365) or (125/366) of the days. To the nearest 1%, both equal 34%. A) 34 B) 33 C) 13 D) 3	5. A
6. 444 444 444 = 4 × 111 111 111 = 111 × 4 004 004 = 444 × 1 001 001. A) 4 B) 11 C) 111 D) 444	6. B
7. The 3 consecutive integers are 2001, 2002, and 2003. A) 1999 B) 2000 C) 2001 D) 2005	7. C
8. Both sides have 2 decimal places, so only multiply by 1. A) 0.01 B) 0.1 C) 1 D) 10	8. C
9. The reciprocal of a positive prime number is between 0 and 1. A) odd B) even C) prime D) positive	9. D
10. Since 175÷7 = 25 is the only whole number, choice D is correct. A) $\frac{135}{7}$ B) $\frac{145}{9}$ C) $\frac{155}{11}$ D) $\frac{175}{7}$	10. D
11. *Work backwards.* An equilateral △ with side 12 has perimeter 3×12 = 36. A square with perimeter 36 has side 36÷4 = 9. A) 3 B) 9 C) 16 D) 36	11. B
12. 1 + 2×3 + 4 = 1 + 6+4 = 1+10 = 1 + 2×5 = 1 + 2×(3+2). A) 2 B) 4 C) 5 D) 7	12. A
13. The cost of 100 gumdrops is 100×2¢ = 200¢. The cost of 50 gumballs is 50×1¢ = 50¢. The difference is 150¢ = $1.50. A) $1.00 B) $1.50 C) $2.00 D) $3.50	13. B
14. $\dfrac{7+8}{(7\times7)+(7\times8)} = \dfrac{(7+8)}{(7)\times(7+8)} = \dfrac{1}{7} = \dfrac{1}{7} + 0.$ A) 0 B) $\frac{1}{7}$ C) $\frac{1}{8}$ D) 1	14. A
15. $4^2 \times 5^2 \times 6^2 = (4\times5\times6)^2 = (120)^2.$ A) 15 B) 25 C) 77 D) 120	15. D

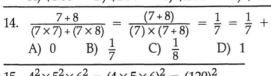

Go on to the next page ⫸ **8**

16. Average angle measure = sum/3 = 180°/3 = 60°. A) 30° B) 45° C) 60° D) 90°	16. C
17. $10^5 \times 10^5 = 10^{10} = 10\,000\,000\,000$; $99\,999 \times 99\,999$ is slightly less. A) 11 B) 10 C) 8 D) 5	17. B
18. Order of operations: $9 \times 9 + 9 \div 9 - 9 = 81 + 1 - 9 = 73$. A) 73 B) 45 C) 9 D) 1	18. A

19. Saturday is 6 days after Sunday
    and 3 days before Tuesday.
    A) Mon.   B) Wed.   C) Thurs.   D) Sat.
	19.
	D

20. 0.2% of 2% of 20 = $0.002 \times 0.02 \times 20 = 0.0008$. A) 0.0008 B) 0.008 C) 0.08 D) 8.0	20. A
21. #s could be ½ & ¼, or –½ & –¼, or any two #s with same sign. A) positive B) negative C) 0 D) a fraction	21. C
22. $3^9 \div 9^3 = 3^9 \div (3^2)^3 = 3^9 \div 3^6 = 3^3$, so the remainder is 0. A) $3 - 3$ B) 3×3 C) $3 + 9$ D) 3×9	22. A

23. Since 1-10 uses 10 digits, while 11-20, 21-30, 31-40, 41-50 all use
    19 digits, the total number of digits used is $10 + (4 \times 19) = 86$.
    A) 90   B) 86   C) 50   D) 45
	23.
	B

24. If 3 out of 4 people are into hot soup, then
    ¾ × 700 = 525 of 700 are into hot soup.
    A) 475   B) 500   C) 525   D) 550
	24.
	C

25. In D, 3006 is about half of 6003;
    D is the only such choice.
    A) 2991   B) 3002   C) 4008   D) 6003
	25.
	D

26. $\left(\frac{1}{4}\right)^2 = \frac{1}{16} < \frac{1}{4}$. A) $\sqrt{\frac{1}{4}} = \frac{1}{2}$ B) $\frac{1}{4} \div \frac{1}{4} = 1$ C) $\left(\frac{1}{4}\right)^2 = \frac{1}{16}$ D) $1 \div \frac{1}{4} = 4$	26. C
27. If $a \diamond b = a \times b + b^2$, then $8 \diamond 6 = 8 \times 6 + 6^2 = 48 + 36 = 84$. A) 100 B) 84 C) 54 D) 48	27. B
28. The additive inverse is negative, and (pos.)(neg.) = neg. A) greater than 1 B) 1 C) 0 D) less than 0	28. D

29. Since each straight line side contains only two vertices, only
    two points lie on the same line right now. If 4 people move to
    that line, then all 6 people could stand in a straight line.
    A) 5   B) 4   C) 3   D) 2
	29.
	B

Go on to the next page ▐▐▐➡ **8**

30. The least common multiple of 2, 3, 4, and 5 is 60. Since 60 goes into 1000 exactly 16⅔ times, there are 16 such numbers. A) 8 　　 B) 9 　　　 C) 16 　　　 D) 17	30. C
31. For choice A: $-5 \times 25 = -125$; for choice B: $-1 \times 21 = -21$; for choice C: $1 \times 19 = 19$; the answer is D. A) -125 　 B) -21 　 C) 19 　 D) 60	31. D
32. Ratio of the # of secs in 45 mins to the # of secs in one hour is $(45 \times 60):(60 \times 60) = 45:60 = 3:4$. A) 1:2 　 B) 1:4 　 C) 3:4 　 D) 4:3	32. C
33. $50\% + 50\% = 100\% = 1 = 0.02 \times 50 = 2\%$ of 50. A) 1% 　 B) 2% 　 C) 50% 　 D) 100%	33. B
34. The difference between 1 and its reciprocal, 1, is 0. This is the smallest possible difference. A) 0 　 B) $\frac{1}{5}$ 　 C) $\frac{7}{12}$ 　 D) $\frac{3}{2}$	34. A
35. Examine a special case. Suppose my island had 100 people. Then 40%, or 40, represents 50% of the # shipwrecked on your island; so you have 80 people. The ratio of the numbers of shipwrecked people is $100:80 = 125\%$. A) 80% 　 B) 90% 　 C) 120% 　 D) 125%	35. D
36. The average of all 32 grades was $(80 \times 12 + 70 \times 20) \div 32 =$ $(960 + 1400) \div 32 = 2360 \div 32 = 73.75$. A) 72.25 　 B) 73.75 　 C) 74.75 　 D) 75.00	36. B
37. $\left(\sqrt{\sqrt{x}}\right)^4 = (\sqrt{x})^2 = x$. 　　 A) $\sqrt{x}$ 　 B) x 　 C) x^2 　 D) x^4	37. B
38. Area $= 72 \text{ cm}^2 = (8 \text{ cm}) \times (9 \text{ cm})$, and perimeter $= 34 \text{ cm} = 2 \times (8 \text{ cm} + 9 \text{ cm})$. The difference is $9 \text{ cm} - 8 \text{ cm} = 1 \text{ cm}$. A) 1 cm 　　 B) 6 cm 　　 C) 18 cm 　　 D) 38 cm	38. A
39. Let's guess and check. If the small circle has $r = 1$, then the large circle has $R = 3$, and $\pi R^2 - 3\pi r^2 = 9\pi - 3\pi = 6\pi$. If $r = 2$, then $R = 6$, and $\pi R^2 - 3\pi r^2 = 36\pi - 12\pi = 24\pi$. Thus, $r = 2$ and $\pi r^2 = 4\pi$. A) 12π 　 B) 9π 　 C) 4π 　 D) π	39. C
40. $\dfrac{2^{49}}{2^{50}} + \dfrac{2^{48}}{2^{50}} + \dfrac{2^{47}}{2^{50}} + \ldots + \dfrac{1}{2^{50}} = \dfrac{(2^{49} + 2^{48} + 2^{47} + \ldots + 2^1) + 1}{2^{50}}$. A) 0 　　　 B) 1 　　　 C) 2^{50} 　　　 D) $1 + 2^{50}$	40. B

The end of the contest ✍ **8**

Visit our Web site at http://www.mathleague.com

EIGHTH GRADE MATHEMATICS CONTEST

Math League Press, P.O. Box 17, Tenafly, New Jersey 07670–0017

Information & Solutions

Tuesday, February 18 or 25, 2003

Contest Information

8

- **Solutions** Turn the page for detailed contest solutions (written in the question boxes) and letter answers (written in the *Answers* column to the right of each question).

- **Scores** Please remember that *this is a contest, not a test*—and there is no "passing" or "failing" score. Few students score as high as 30 points (75% correct). Students with half that, 15 points, *deserve commendation!*

- **Answers & Rating Scale** Turn to page 144 for the letter answers to each question and the rating scale for this contest.

1. The thousandths' digit of 0.0409 is 0, so round down to 0.04. A) 0.0401 B) 0.040 C) 0.041 D) 0.04	1. D
2. The reciprocal of 0.5 = 1/2 is 2. The sum is 0.5 + 2.0 = 2.5. A) 0 B) 1 C) 2 D) 2.5	2. D
3. In the product $2\,000\,000 \times 5\,000\,000$, the first digit is a 1. Since every other digit is a 0, I ate only 1 doughnut. A) 1 B) 2 C) 7 D) 10	3. A
4. Since $1^2 = 1$, and since $1 < 2(1) = 2$, the answer is 1. A) 2 B) 1 C) 0 D) –2	4. B
5. $25 \times \left(\frac{1}{4} + \frac{1}{4} + \frac{1}{4} + \frac{1}{4}\right) = 25 \times 1 = 25.$ A) 0.25 B) 1 C) 25 D) 100	5. C
6. Since $210 \div 2 = 105$ is odd, 105 is the largest odd factor of 210. A) 21 B) 63 C) 105 D) 209	6. C
7. $111 - 11 = 100$. Answer = $1111 - 111 = 1000$. A) 10 B) 11 C) 100 D) 1000	7. D
8. 31 days = 28 days + 3 days; 28 days before Tues. is Tues., and 3 days before Tues. is Sat. A) Thurs. B) Fri. C) Sat. D) Sun.	8. C
9. Since $0.12 - 0.34$ is negative, it's less than 0.12×0.34. A) $0.12 - 0.34$ B) $0.12 + 0.34$ C) 0.1234 D) 12×34	9. A
10. B gives the correct order of operations: first multiply, then add. A) $(7+8) \times 7 + 8$ B) $7 + (8 \times 7) + 8$ C) $7 + 8 \times (7+8)$ D) $(7+8) \times (7+8)$	10. B
11. Both legs can be 5, but the hypotenuse must be the longest side. A) 3 sides B) 2 sides C) 1 side D) 0 sides	11. B
12. 100 dollars + 100 quarters + 100 dimes + 100 nickels = $100 + $25 + $10 + $5 = $140. A) $140 B) $145 C) $175 D) $400	12. A
13. Since quotient is tripled, divisor must be tripled. A) 1 B) 6 C) 9 D) 27	13. C
14. $(1/4)^2 = (1/4) \times (1/4) = 1/16$. A) $\left(\frac{1}{4}\right)^2$ B) $\frac{60}{120}$ C) 0.5 D) $\sqrt{\frac{1}{4}}$	14. A

Go on to the next page ⅢⅢ➡ **8**

15. $\frac{1}{3}\times9\times\frac{1}{6}\times6\times\frac{1}{9}\times3 = \frac{1}{9}\times9\times\frac{1}{6}\times6\times\frac{1}{3}\times3 = 1$. A) 9 B) 3 C) 1 D) $\frac{1}{6}$	15. C
16. Their average = sum ÷ 4 = (1/2) ÷ 4 = 1/8. A) one-eighth B) one-fourth C) one-half D) 2	16. A
17. The sides cannot be 12, 12, 24 since the sum of any two sides must exceed the third. The sides are 12, 24, 24. A) 36 B) 42 C) 60 D) 72	17. C
18. $6\times12\times18\times24 = (2\times3)(2^2\times3)(2\times3^2)(2^3\times3) = 2^7\times3^5$. A) $2^6\times3^6$ B) $2^7\times3^6$ C) $2^6\times3^5$ D) $2^7\times3^5$	18. D
19. $0.20\times30 = 6.00 = 0.30\times20$. A) 0.2 B) 20 C) 2% D) 200%	19. B
20. $7\times0.25 = 7\times\frac{1}{4} = 7 \div 4$. A) 0.25 B) 4 C) 25 D) 100	20. B
21. 2 divides all evens. 1, not a prime, is odd, whole, and positive. A) whole B) odd C) even D) positive	21. C
22. Both Sue and Dan are older than Ann, who is older than Bob. Sue and Dan could be the same age. A) Bob & Sue B) Dan & Bob C) Ann & Bob D) Sue & Dan 	22. D
23. $(0.1)^{10} = (1/10)^{10} = 1^{10}/10^{10} = 1/10^{10}$. A) 1 B) $\frac{1}{10}$ C) $\frac{1}{100}$ D) $\frac{1}{10^{10}}$	23. D
24. 139 min. = 120 min. + 19 min. = 2 hr. + 19 min. A) 10:39 P.M. B) 10:49 P.M. C) 10:59 P.M. D) 11:19 P.M.	24. B
25. $\frac{2^2}{4^2} + \frac{4^2}{2^2} = \left(\frac{2}{4}\right)^2 + \left(\frac{4}{2}\right)^2 = \left(\frac{1}{2}\right)^2 + 2^2$. A) $\frac{1}{2^2}$ B) 0 C) 2^2 D) 4^2	25. A
26. $10\% = 0.1 = 1/10 = 1 \div 10$. A) 1 B) 10 C) 100 D) 10 000	26. A
27. (24 kittens):(18 puppies) = (4 kittens):(3 puppies) = (32 kittens):(24 puppies). A) 18 B) 24 C) 32 D) 36	27. C
28. If my phone's extension number has 3 digits, the sum of its digits can be at most $3\times9 = 27$. A) 3 B) 4 C) 5 D) 7	28. A

Go on to the next page ▐▐▐▶ **8**

29. $\frac{3}{4}:3 = \left(\frac{4}{3}\times\frac{4}{3}\times\frac{3}{4}\right):\left(\frac{4}{3}\times\frac{4}{3}\times 3\right) = \frac{4}{3}:\frac{16}{3}$. A) $\frac{9}{4}$ B) $\frac{16}{3}$ C) 4 D) 12	29. B
30. The product of a number and its additive inverse is 0 or negative. A) 0 B) –1 C) 1 D) –4	30. C
31. 15 crows nested either alone or paired with 1 other. To use all 8 nests, 14 paired crows occupied 7 nests, and 1 crow nested alone. A) 0 B) 1 C) 2 D) 3	31. B
32. For the smallest possible difference, use the numbers 1, 2, 3, 4, and 5. Their sum is 15, the largest of them is 5, and $15-5 = 10$. A) 0 B) 2 C) 5 D) 10	32. D
33. $2^2\times 2^4 = (2\times 2)\times 2^4 = 2\times(2\times 2^4) = 2\times 2^5$. A) 2^5 B) 2^6 C) 2^7 D) 2^8	33. A
34. At 90 pages/hr, I can read one 270-page book in 3 hrs and 2 such books in 6 hrs. A) 2 B) 3 C) 15 D) 18	34. A
35. $2\times 4\times 6\times 8\times 10 = 2^8\times 3\times 5$. The perfect squares have even exponents: $2^8 = 16^2$, $2^6 = 8^2$, $2^4 = 4^2$, $2^2 = 2^2$, and $2^0 = 1^2$. A) 5 B) 4 C) 3 D) 2	35. A
36. $2\pi(4/2\pi) = 4$, so radius $= 4/2\pi = 2/\pi$. Area $= \pi(4/\pi^2) = 4/\pi$. A) $\frac{4}{\pi}$ B) $\frac{16}{\pi}$ C) 4π D) 16π	36. A
37. Since $3^2+4^2 = 5^2$, if two sides of a right $\triangle$ are 3 and 5, the 3rd side could be 4. A) 10 B) 11 C) 12 D) 13	37. C
38. Each face of a cube has a perimeter of 36, so each edge is $36\div 4 = 9$. The volume $= 9^3 = 729$. A) 36 B) 81 C) 216 D) 729	38. D
39. $2.7\times 10^{28} = 27\times 10^{27} = 3^3\times(10^9)^3 = (3\times 10^9)^3 = n^3$. A) 2.7×10^{27} B) 2.7×10^{28} C) 2.7×10^{29} D) 2.7×10^{30}	39. B
40. Least possible sum $= 1+2+...+999+1000$. Avg. # $=$ exact middle $=$ avg of 500 & 501 $= 500.5$. Thus, least sum $= 500.5\times 1000 = 500\,500$. A) $499\,000$ B) $499\,500$ C) $500\,000$ D) $500\,500$	40. D

The end of the contest ✍ **8**

Visit our Web site at http://www.mathleague.com

Information & Solutions

Tuesday, February 17 or 24, 2004

Contest Information

8

- **Solutions** Turn the page for detailed contest solutions (written in the question boxes) and letter answers (written in the *Answers* column to the right of each question).

- **Scores** Please remember that *this is a contest, not a test*—and there is no "passing" or "failing" score. Few students score as high as 30 points (75% correct). Students with half that, 15 points, *deserve commendation!*

- **Answers & Rating Scale** Turn to page 145 for the letter answers to each question and the rating scale for this contest.

103

1. $(99-98) \times (88-87) \times (77-76) \times (66-65) = 1 \times 1 \times 1 \times 1 = 1.$ A) 0 B) 1 C) 4 D) 11		1. B
2. $1^2 + (-1)^2 - 1^2 = 1+1-1 = 1.$ A) 1 B) -1 C) 0 D) 3		2. A
3. Multiply each choice by 4 to find the perimeter. Since $4 \times 0.75 = 3$, the correct answer is choice B. A) 0.50 B) 0.75 C) 1.00 D) 1.50	**IN CASE OF** **PANIC** ⬇	3. B
4. $7 \times (3+4+5+6+7+8+9) = 7 \times 42.$ A) 7 B) 14 C) 42 D) 49		4. C
5. $\frac{3}{12} = \frac{1}{4} = \frac{4}{16}.$ A) 4 B) 3 C) $\frac{1}{4}$ D) 25%		5. A
6. The largest angle in an obtuse triangle is greater than 90°. A) equilateral B) acute C) obtuse D) right		6. C
7. $30 \times 25¢ + 30 \times 10¢ + 30 \times 5¢ + 30 \times 1¢ = \$12.30; 30 \times 50¢ = \$15.$ Paying with 30 half-dollars overpays by \$15 - \$12.30 = \$2.70. A) \$2.30 B) \$2.70 C) \$3.00 D) \$3.20		7. B
8. Since $3999¢ \div 39¢ \approx 102.5$, I can buy *at most* 102 trinkets. A) 100 B) 101 C) 102 D) 103		8. C
9. $8765 \times 4321 = 37\,873\,565$, a number whose tens' digit is 6. A) 5 B) 6 C) 7 D) 8		9. B
10. 1 grain weighs 0.01 g, so 100 grains weigh 1 g. Since 1 kg = 1000 g, 1 kg contains $1000 \times 100 = 100\,000$ grains. A) 100 B) 1000 C) 10 000 D) 100 000		10. D
11. $120 \div 2 = 180 \div 3 = 240 \div 4 = 60 = 360 \div 6.$ A) 5 B) 6 C) 8 D) 12		11. B
12. The additive inverse of $\frac{1}{2}$ is $-\frac{1}{2}$. A) negative B) whole C) prime D) positive		12. A
13. If May 1 is a Saturday, then May 2, May 9, May 16, May 23, and May 30 are all Sundays. Kay will have 5 sundaes in May. A) 2 B) 3 C) 4 D) 5		13. D
14. The sum of two odd numbers can never be odd. A) 124 B) 142 C) 214 D) 241		14. D
15. If twice a number is 96, then the number is 48; $48/3 = 16.$ A) 16 B) 32 C) 48 D) 64		15. A

Go on to the next page ⮕ **8**

16. The gcfs of the choices are 3, 9, 6, and 3, respectively.
    A) 33, 90   B) 36, 63   C) 66, 96   D) 99, 39

16. B

17. Try an example: 20 + 20 + 20 + 20 + 20 = 100, and
    22 + 22 + 22 + 22 + 22 = 110.
    A) 1   B) 2   C) 10   D) 50

17. C

18. I need $32 \times 3 = 96$ minutes to draw, but I rest
    31 times between sketches, and $31 \times 2 = 62$
    mins. Total time = 158 mins. = 2 hr 38 mins.
    A) 4:37   B) 4:38   C) 4:39   D) 4:40

18. B

19. 3 mins. = (90 mins. ÷ 30) is (100% ÷ 30) = (10/3)%.
    A) $\frac{1}{3}$ B) $\frac{1}{2}$ C) $\frac{10}{3}$ D) 5

19. C

20. $(100 + 88) \times (100 - 88) = 188 \times 12$, and this equals $100^2 - 88^2$.
    A) 0   B) 100^2 C) 2×8800 D) $100^2 - 88^2$

20. D

21. Adding 30 triples my age, so 30 is double my age. My age is 15.
    A) 15   B) 12   C) 10   D) 9

21. A

22. Since $\frac{38}{57} = \frac{2}{3}$, tripling both sides gives us $3 \times \frac{38}{57} = 3 \times \frac{2}{3} = 2$.
    A) 2   B) 19   C) 38   D) 57

22. A

23. Since $1^{25} = 1$, 25% = 0.25, and 1/25 = 0.04, choice D is greatest.
    A) 1^{25} B) 25%   C) $\frac{1}{25}$ D) 2.5

23. D

24. AC must be less than 18, so the perimeter is less than 18+18.
    A) 33   B) 34   C) 35   D) 36

24. D

25. If you add 1, 2, 3, . . . , 100, and I add 2, 3, 4, . . . , 100, then
    the least possible difference between your sum and mine is 1.
    A) 0   B) 1   C) 99   D) 100

25. B

26. Since 1 km = 1000 m, a ball with a 5 m
    circumference needs 1000÷5 turns.
    A) 400   B) 314
    C) 200   D) 100

26. C

27. The square root of 4^4 is 4^2,
    and the square root of 4^2 is 4.
    A) 4^2 B) 4^3 C) 4^4 D) 4^8

27. C

28. The reciprocal of $\frac{2}{3} \times \frac{5}{6} = \frac{10}{18}$ is $\frac{18}{10} = \frac{3}{2} \times \frac{6}{5}$.
    A) $\frac{2}{3} \times \frac{5}{6}$ B) $\frac{2}{3} \times \frac{6}{5}$ C) $\frac{3}{2} \times \frac{5}{6}$ D) $\frac{3}{2} \times \frac{6}{5}$

28. D

29. The smallest such sum is 6 + 12 + 18 + 24 + 30 = 90.
    A) 60   B) 90   C) 130   D) 160

29. B

Go on to the next page ⫸ **8**

30. Since $18 = 2 \times (1 + 8)$, the two-digit number is 18. The sum of the digits of 18 is 9.

    A) 9   B) 12   C) 18   D) 36

    30.

    A

31. From the top of a step to the top of the step above is $25 \text{ cm} + 2 \text{ cm} = 27 \text{ cm}$. From the top of step 1 to the top of step 6 is $5 \times 27 \text{ cm} = 135 \text{ cm}$. It's another 25 cm from the top of step 6 to the bottom of step 7. The distance from step 1 to step 7 is $135 \text{ cm} + 25 \text{ cm} = 160 \text{ cm}$.

    A) 135 cm   B) 137 cm   C) 160 cm   D) 162 cm

    31.

    C

32. The 3 integers must add up to 9. If we use 1, 2, and 6, their product is $1 \times 2 \times 6 = 12$.

    A) 9   B) 12   C) 24   D) 27

    32.

    B

33. $*2543* = 2 \times 3 + 5 \times 4 = 6 + 20 = 26$.

    A) 14   B) 22   C) 26   D) 120

    33.

    C

34. Using 3 & 1, sum $= 3+1 = \mathbf{4}$, difference $= 3 - 1 = \mathbf{2}$, and quotient $= \mathbf{4} \div \mathbf{2} = 2$, so it's D.

    A) 0   B) 0.5   C) 1   D) 2

    34.

    D

35. (# mins in 1 sec) $\div$ (# secs in 1 min) $= \dfrac{1}{60} \div 60 = 1/3600 < 1$.

    A) 3600   B) 60   C) 1   D) less than 1

    35.

    D

36. $(\dfrac{1}{111} \div 111) \times 100\% = \dfrac{1}{111^2} \times 100\% = 0.008\%$ (to the nearest 0.001%).

    A) 0.008%   B) 0.009%   C) 0.901%   D) 1.000%

    36.

    A

37. $\sqrt{\sqrt{9^{16}}} = \sqrt{9^8} = 9^4$.   A) 3^2 B) 9^2 C) 9^4 D) 9^8

    37. C

38. The easiest approach is to try an example: 10 km in 10 mins. is 1 km/min., but 12 km in 8 mins. is 1.5 km/min.

    A) 140   B) 150   C) 160   D) 170

    38.

    B

39. For parts of the year for ages 8 & 9, her age in months > 100. Similarly, for ages 83 to 99, her age in months > 1000 all or part of the time. In all, there are 19 years.

    A) 16   B) 17   C) 18   D) 19

    39.

    D

40. Each of the larger integers is 2004 more than the corresponding smaller one. The total difference between them is 2004×2004.

    A) 2004   B) 4008   C) 2004^2 D) 4008^2

    40.

    C

The end of the contest ✍ **8**

Visit our Web site at http://www.mathleague.com

Information & Solutions

February 15 or 22, 2005

Contest Information

8

- **Solutions** Turn the page for detailed contest solutions (written in the question boxes) and letter answers (written in the *Answers* column to the right of each question).

- **Scores** Please remember that *this is a contest, not a test*—and there is no "passing" or "failing" score. Few students score as high as 30 points (75% correct). Students with half that, 15 points, *deserve commendation!*

- **Answers & Rating Scale** Turn to page 146 for the letter answers to each question and the rating scale for this contest.

1. Subtract 1000 from each: $110-020$. A) 102 B) 101 C) 90 D) 20	1. D
2. Each side of the square has length $4 \div 4 = 1$. The square's area $= 1^2 = 1$. A) 1 B) 4 C) 8 D) 16	2. A
3. $300 \div 200 = 3/2 = 1 \times (3/2) = 1 \div (2/3)$. A) $\frac{1}{3}$ B) $\frac{1}{2}$ C) $\frac{2}{3}$ D) $\frac{3}{2}$	3. C
4. Five-fourths $= 5/4$, which is an improper fraction. A) $\frac{4}{5}$ B) $1\frac{1}{4}$ C) 1.25 D) $\frac{5}{4}$	4. D
5. $(2005-2005)-2004 = -2004$. A) 1 B) -2004 C) -2005 D) -2006	5. B
6. 120 seconds $= 2$ minutes, so the time is 12:02 A.M. A) 12:02 P.M. B) 12:02 A.M. C) 2 P.M. D) 2 A.M.	6. B
7. $24 \div 4 \times 2 + 4 = [(24 \div 4) \times 2] + 4 = (6 \times 2) + 4 = 12 + 4 = 16$. A) 1 B) 7 C) 16 D) 36	7. C
8. $\frac{1}{2} \times 4 = 2$, so its reciprocal is $\frac{1}{2} = 2 \times \frac{1}{4}$. A) $2 \times \frac{1}{4}$ B) $\frac{1}{2} \times 4$ C) $\frac{1}{2} \times \frac{1}{4}$ D) 2×4	8. A
9. $1.000-0.995 = 0.005$; $1.000-0.990 = 0.010$; $1.010-1.000 = 0.010$; $1.100-1.000 = 0.100$. A) 0.995 B) 0.99 C) 1.01 D) 1.1	9. A
10. By definition, 1 is *not* a prime, so the sum is $2+3+5+7 = 17$. A) 15 B) 16 C) 17 D) 18	10. C
11. $2 \times \frac{1}{2} \times 4 \times \frac{1}{4} \times 6 \times \frac{1}{6} = (2 \times \frac{1}{2}) \times (4 \times \frac{1}{4}) \times (6 \times \frac{1}{6}) = 1 \times 1 \times 1 = 1$. A) 1 B) 6 C) 12 D) 24	11. A
12. The sum of the measures of each possible pair of angles is 120°, so each angle is 60°. Therefore, triangle T *must* be equilangular. A) scalene B) right C) obtuse D) equiangular	12. D
13. If Sunday is cloudy, then Tuesday, Thursday, and Saturday may also be cloudy. I wear my headphones at most 4 times in a week. A) 3 B) 4 C) 5 D) 6	13. B
14. Of the choices below, D has the largest value. A) 7 B) $(-1)^2 = 1$ C) $(-2)^2 = 4$ D) $(-3)^2 = 9$	14. D
15. $9000\% + 900\% + 90\% + 9\% = 90 + 9 + 0.9 + 0.09 = 99.99$. A) 9999 B) 999.9 C) 99.99 D) 0.9999	15. C

Go on to the next page IIII➡ **8**

16. A dealer paid Bunny Fabergé 50¢ for each of his eggs. The dealer then sold each egg for 50 quarters. For each penny Fabergé got, the dealer got 25¢, so Fabergé got 4¢ on the dollar, which is 4%.
A) 2%   B) 4%   C) 25%   D) 50%

16.

B

17. Since $\sqrt{256} = 16$, $\sqrt{\sqrt{\sqrt{256}}} = \sqrt{\sqrt{16}} = \sqrt{4} = 2$.
A) 2   B) 4   C) 8   D) 16

17.
A

18. $0.3 \times 0.4 = 0.12$.   A) 12%   B) 120%   C) 1200%   D) 12000%

18. A

19. The 4 whole numbers factors of 10 are 1, 2, 5, and 10.
A) 30   B) 24   C) 12   D) 10

19.
D

20. $1/5 = 0.2 < 0.33 < 0.4 = 2/5$; 0.33 closer to 2/5.
A) 0.2   B) 0.3   C) $\frac{2}{5}$ D) $\frac{3}{5}$

20.
C

21. I had 4 pennies; need 3 coins = 45¢, so I need 1 quarter; 2 coins = 20¢ are 2 dimes.
A) 0   B) 1   C) 2   D) 7

21.
A

22. 1.5 m $+ 60 \times 0.01$ m $+ 0.02 \times 1000$ m $= 22.1$ m.
A) 0.221 m   B) 2.21 m   C) 22.1 m   D) 221 m

22.
C

23. There are four even factors of 222. They are 2, 6, 74, and 222.
A) 111   B) 4   C) 3   D) 1

23.
B

24. The average of 1, 2, . . . , 98, 99 is the middle number, 50.
A) 49.00   B) 49.50   C) 49.75   D) 50.00

24.
D

25. In the large circle, if $r = 2$, then the large circle's area would be 4π. Small circle then has $r = 1$, so $A = \pi$. That's 25% of 4π.
A) 20   B) 25   C) 40   D) 50

25.
B

26. If 2/3 cup of fish food feeds 8 goldfish, then 1/3 cup feeds 4 fish, and 1 cup feeds 12 fish. Thus, 4 cups feed 48 fish.
A) 12   B) 24   C) 36   D) 48

26.
D

27. The square of an odd number is always odd.
A) prime   B) odd   C) even   D) zero

27.
B

28. Since the reciprocal of $\frac{1}{x^3}$ is x^3, $4x = x^3$. The value $x = 2$ works.
A) $\frac{1}{8}$ B) $\frac{1}{2}$ C) 2   D) 8

28.
C

Go on to the next page ||||➡   **8**

29. $2^{10} \times 2^{10} = 2^{10+10} = 2^{20}$. A) 2^{20} B) 2^{100} C) 4^{20} D) 4^{100}	29. A
30. Divide by 60 to get # minutes. Repeat to get # hours. Divide result by 24 to get # days ≈ 11.57. A) January 11 B) January 12 C) February 1 D) February 2	30. B
31. As in 29 above, $16^8 \times 16^8 = 16^{16}$, so $\sqrt{16^{16}} = 16^8$. A) 4^4 B) 4^8 C) 16^4 D) 16^8	31. D
32. If 2005 fractions each have an even numerator and an odd denominator of 1, their product would be an even integer. A) even B) odd C) prime D) 2005	32. A
33. In a $\triangle$, the sum of the 2 smaller side-lengths must be greater than the 3rd side-length. Thus, the perimeter $\leq 3+4+6 = 13$. A) 11 B) 12 C) 13 D) 14	33. C
34. $10\,000^{9999} = (10^4)^{9999} = 10^{39\,996}$. That's 1 followed by 39 996 zeroes! A) 9999 B) 10 000 C) 39 996 D) 39 997	34. D
35. The 2 small and 2 large $\triangle$s are shown: A) 2 B) 3 C) 4 D) 5	35. C
36. The 2000 integers $-999, -998, \ldots , 998, 999, 1000$ have a sum of 1000. The digit-sum of the largest integer used is $1+0+0+0 = 1$. A) 1 B) 2 C) 9 D) 27	36. A
37. The 9 factors divisible by 4 are 4, 8, 16, 20, 40, 80, 100, 200, & 400. A) 4 B) 8 C) 9 D) 10	37. C
38. Notice that $0^2 = 0$ and that $1^2 = 1$. These are the only two integers which are equal to their own squares. A) zero B) one C) two D) three	38. C
39. The hr. hand moves $30°$ in 1 hr. and $(22/60) \times 30° = 11°$ in 22 mins. A) $10°$ B) $11°$ C) $21°$ D) $22°$	39. B
40. The product includes several multiples of 10; it's divisible by 100. A) 4 B) 6 C) 8 D) 0	40. D

The end of the contest ✍ **8**

Information & Solutions

February 21 or 28, 2006

Contest Information

8

- **Solutions** Turn the page for detailed contest solutions (written in the question boxes) and letter answers (written in the *Answers* column to the right of each question).

- **Scores** Please remember that *this is a contest, not a test*—and there is no "passing" or "failing" score. Few students score as high as 30 points (75% correct). Students with half that, 15 points, *deserve commendation!*

- **Answers & Rating Scale** Turn to page 147 for the letter answers to each question and the rating scale for this contest.

1. By calculator or by hand, $11\,011 - 1001 = 10\,010$.
   A) 1001   B) $10\,001$ C) $10\,010$ D) $10\,101$

   1. **C**

2. Earth is the 5th largest of 9 planets, so 4 are larger and 4 are smaller. The ratio of the number larger to the number smaller is 4:4, or 1:1.
   A) 1:1   B) 2:1   C) 4:5   D) 5:4

   2. **A**

3. Try some: $7 \times 8 = 56$; $8 \times 9 = 72$; $9 \times 10 = 90$; **$10 \times 11 = 110$**.
   A) 65   B) 80   C) 96   D) 110

   3. **D**

4. Two perpendicular lines intersect in 1 point, as seen here: $\perp$.
   A) 0 points   B) 1 point   C) 2 points   D) 4 points

   4. **B**

5. Since 20, 10, and 4 are not prime, the prime factorization is D.
   A) 2×20 B) $2 \times 2 \times 10$ C) $2 \times 4 \times 5$ D) $2 \times 2 \times 2 \times 5$

   5. **D**

6. Each of A, B, D is the sum of a positive integer and its reciprocal.
   A) $12 + \frac{1}{12}$ B) $6 + \frac{1}{6}$ C) $4 + \frac{1}{3}$ D) $2 + \frac{1}{2}$

   6. **C**

7. $\frac{1}{2} \times \frac{1}{2} = \frac{1}{4}$, and $\frac{1}{4} = \frac{1}{2} \div 2$.   A) 4   B) 2   C) $\frac{1}{2}$ D) $\frac{1}{4}$

   7. **B**

8. A $\triangle$ may have one angle $\geq 90°$; the other two must be acute.
   A) 0   B) 1   C) 2   D) 3

   8. **C**

9. $0.5 \times 0.5 = 0.25$, which is 0.25×1.
   A) 1   B) 0.75
   C) 0.25   D) 10

   9. **A**

10. There are 90 2-digit positive integers. Nine are divisible by 10: $10, 20, 30, \ldots, 90$. So there are $90 - 9 = 81$ eggs in my basket.
    A) 78   B) 79   C) 80   D) 81

    10. **D**

11. The solution to $3^2 + 3^2 = 6^2 - \underline{?}$ is 18, and $18 = 3^2 + 3^2$.
    A) 2^2 B) 3^2 C) $2^2 + 2^2$ D) $3^2 + 3^2$

    11. **D**

12. Examples like $2 \times 6 = 12$ and $10 \times 30 = 300$ aren't divisible by 8.
    A) 1   B) 2   C) 4   D) 8

    12. **D**

13. One photo's area is 24. The board's is 24×40. The quotient is 40.
    A) 40   B) 24   C) 20   D) 16

    13. **A**

14. $\frac{2}{3} + \frac{3}{2} + \frac{2}{3} + \frac{3}{2} + \frac{2}{3} = (\frac{2}{3} + \frac{2}{3} + \frac{2}{3}) + (\frac{3}{2} + \frac{3}{2}) = \frac{6}{3} + \frac{6}{2} = 2 + 3$.
    A) $3 + 2$ B) $3 - 2$ C) $3 \div 2$ D) $2 \div 3$

    14. **A**

Go on to the next page ⫸ **8**

15. As seen below, choice D is the least.
    A) $(2) \div (1) - 1 = 2 - 1 = 1$ B) $1 + (1 \times 1) - 1 = 1 + 1 - 1 = 1$
    C) $1 + ((1) \times 1 - 1) = 1 + (1 - 1) = 1 + 0 = 1$ D) $(1 + 1) \times (0) = 0$

15. D

16. The average is $(10 - 10 + 5 - 5 + 100) \div 5 = (0 + 100) \div 5 = 20$.
    A) 0   B) 20   C) 25   D) 100

16. B

17. The length of 1 piece is $(40 \div 4)$ m $= 10$ m. The rectangle's perimeter is 10 m. The sum of the width and length is half this, 5 m.
    A) 5 m   B) 10 m   C) 20 m   D) 40 m

17. A

18. $0 \times 1 = \mathbf{0}$, $1 \times 2 = \mathbf{2}$, $2 \times 3 = \mathbf{6}$, so the ones' digit can be 0, 2, or 6.
    A) 1   B) 2   C) 3   D) 4

18. B

19. Righty's drink is 36% soy milk. Lefty's is 4% soy milk. The resulting mixture is half each, so it would be $(36\% + 4\%) \div 2 = 20\%$ soy milk.
    A) 20   B) 32   C) 36   D) 40

19. A

20. The least multiple of 20 that's divisible by both 8 and 12 is 120.
    A) 40   B) 60   C) 120   D) 1920

20. C

21. Use a calculator or: D $= 770\,000 + 350 + 7$; each part is divisible by 7.
    A) 749\,775   B) 735\,814   C) 784\,284   D) 770\,357

21. D

22. $\sqrt{2 \times 4 \times 6 \times 8} = \sqrt{1 \times 2 \times 3 \times 4 \times 2^4} = \sqrt{1 \times 2 \times 3 \times 4} \times 4$.
    A) $\sqrt{2}$ B) 2   C) 4   D) 16

22. C

23. If the average of 8 numbers is 0, their sum $= 8 \times (\text{avg.}) = 0$.
    A) equal 0   B) equal 1   C) exceed 0   D) be negative

23. A

24. 1 hr. $= 60$ mins. $= (60 \times 60)$ secs., and (60×60) mins. $= 60$ hrs.
    A) 24 hours   B) 30 hours   C) 60 hours   D) 90 hours

24. C

25. May 16 is 46 days before July 1 and 15 days after May 1.
    A) May 16   B) May 17   C) June 15   D) June 16

25. A

26. If all 18 diced veggies were among the 20 sliced veggies, then there could be $30 - 20 = 10$ *neither* sliced nor diced.
    A) 2   B) 8   C) 10   D) 12

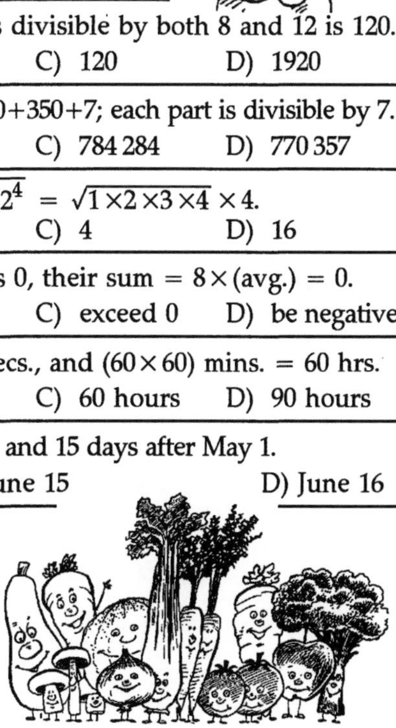

26. C

27. 40% of 100 is 40, of 200 is 80.
    A) 32   B) 120   C) 180   D) 200

27. D

28. $(\frac{7}{8})^7 \div (\frac{8}{7})^8 = (\frac{7}{8})^7 \times (\frac{7}{8})^8 = (\frac{7}{8})^{7+8} = (\frac{7}{8})^{15}$.
    A) 1   B) $\frac{7}{8}$ C) $(\frac{7}{8})^{15}$ D) $(\frac{7}{8})^{56}$

28. C

Go on to the next page ⅢⅢ➡ **8**

113

29. The product of an even and any other integer is always even.
    A) even B) odd C) positive D) divisible by 6

29.
A

30. The circumference is $2\pi \approx 6.283$ and the perimeter is 8.
    Dividing, $2\pi \div 8 \approx 6.283 \div 8 \approx 0.785 \ldots \approx 79\%$.
    A) 75% B) 76% C) 78% D) 79%

30.
D

31. At 30 secs. $= \frac{1}{2}$ min. per page, I'll read the last 200 pages in 100 mins. That leaves *at most* $4\frac{1}{2} \times 60 - 100 = 170$ mins. for the rest.
    A) 50 minutes B) 170 minutes C) 180 minutes D) 200 minutes

31.
B

32. The perimeter of the shaded region consists of the top and bottom sides of the square and the 2 semicircles. The perimeter is $4+2\pi$.
    A) $4+2\pi$ B) $8+2\pi$ C) $4+\pi$ D) $4-\pi$

32.
A

33. The least prime is 2. The sum of all 20 is odd, so we must use a 2.
    A) 5 B) 3 C) 2 D) 1

33.
C

34. The area of my 1×6 sign is 6. If I double each dimension, my new sign is a 2×12 sign whose area is 24 and whose perimeter is $2 \times (2+12) = 28$.
    A) 24 B) 28 C) 48 D) 56

APPLAUSE!

34.
B

35. $\sqrt{1\%} = \sqrt{0.01} = 0.1 = 10\%$.
    A) $\frac{1}{2}\%$ B) 1% C) 10% D) 100%

35.
C

36. The only factors of 3^6 are 1, 3^1, 3^2, 3^3, 3^4, 3^5, and 3^6.
    A) 3 B) 6 C) 7 D) 18

36.
C

37. In 60 minutes, the second hand moves $60 \times 360° = 21\,600°$.
    A) 60° B) 360° C) 3600° D) 21 600°

37.
D

38. The factors of 3 are 1 and 3. Their average is $(1+3) \div 2 = 2$.
    A) 3 B) 4 C) 6 D) 8

38.
A

39. Point B is at $1/3 = 5/15$. Point A is at $1/15$. The average is $(1/15 + 5/15) \div 2 = (6/15) \div 2 = 3/15 = 1/5$.
    A) $\frac{1}{12}$ B) $\frac{1}{6}$ C) $\frac{1}{5}$ D) $\frac{2}{15}$

39.
C

40. $1+3 = 2^2$; $1+3+5 = 3^2$; $1+3+\ldots+4011 = 2006^2 = (2 \times 1003)^2$.
    A) 2×1003^2 B) $2^2 \times 1003^2$ C) 5×1003^2 D) 6×1003^2

40.
B

The end of the contest ✍ **8**

Algebra Course 1 Solutions

2001-2002 through 2005-2006

Information & Solutions

Spring, 2002

Contest Information

- **Solutions** Turn the page for detailed contest solutions (written in the question boxes) and letter answers (written in the *Answers* column to the right of each question).

- **Scores** Please remember that *this is a contest, not a test*—and there is no "passing" or "failing" score. Few students score as high as 30 points (75% correct). Students with half that, 15 points, *deserve commendation!*

- **Answers & Rating Scale** Turn to page 148 for the letter answers to each question and the rating scale for this contest.

1. If $x+2002 = 2001$, then $x = 2001-2002 = -1$.

   A) -1   B) 1   C) -2003   D) 2003

   1.
   A

2. $x + (50\% \text{ of } x) = x + (0.5x) = 1.5x$.

   A) $0.5x$ B) $\frac{x}{2}$ C) $1.5x$ D) $150x$

   2.
   C

3. $(1000 \text{ ants}) \times (5 \text{ hrs}) = 5000 \text{ ant-hrs} = (2500 \text{ ants}) \times (h \text{ hrs})$. Solving, $h = 2$.
   It took the 2500 ants 2 hours.

   A) 1   B) 2   C) 3   D) 4

   3.
   B

4. There are two primes between 50 and 60: 53 and 59. Thus, the number of primes less than 60 is $n+2$.

   A) $n+1$ B) $n+2$ C) $n+3$ D) $n+4$

   4.
   B

5. If $(x + y + z) \div 3 = 18$, then $x + y + z = 3 \times 18 = 54$.

   A) 6   B) 18   C) 36   D) 54

   5.
   D

6. If $n + n = n \times n$, then $2n = n^2$.
   This can be rewritten as
   $n^2 - 2n = 0$ or $n(n - 2) = 0$.
   The only solutions are 0 and 2.

   A) none   B) one   C) two   D) four

   6.
   C

7. $(x+1)^2 - (x-1)^2 = x^2+2x+1 - (x^2-2x+1) = 4x$.

   A) 2   B) -2   C) $4x$ D) $-4x$

   7.
   C

8. Since $2+2 = 4$, $\sqrt{4} + \sqrt{4} = \sqrt{16}$ and $x = 4$.

   A) 2   B) 4   C) 8   D) 12

   8.
   B

9. Since Q's perimeter is 8014,
   $n+(n-1)+(n-2)+(n-3) = 8014$.
   Thus, $4n-6 = 8014$ and
   $n = 2005$.

   A) 2002   B) 2003   C) 2004   D) 2005

   9.
   D

10. Add together the equations $\sqrt{P} + \sqrt{L} = 7$ and $\sqrt{P} - \sqrt{L} = 1$ to obtain $2\sqrt{P} = 8$, $\sqrt{P} = 4$, and $P = 16$.

    A) 3   B) 4   C) 9   D) 16

    10.
    D

Go on to the next page ⟱ **A**

11. $(1-x)(2-x) = (-1)(x-1)(-1)(x-2) = (x-1)(x-2) = 6.$ A) −6 B) −36 C) 6 D) 36	11. C
12. The slope between $(0,0)$ and $(a,b) =$ $b/a =$ slope between $(0,0)$ and $(-a,-b)$.  A) $(-a,b)$ B) $(a,-b)$ C) $(-a,-b)$ D) (a^2,b^2)	12. C
13. Since 0 is an even number that is both greater than −10 and less than +10, the product is 0. A) $38\,400^2$ B) 384^2 C) 384 D) 0	13. D
14. The slope of the line joining $(a,0)$ and $(0,a)$, $a \neq 0$, is $-a/a = -1$, so the correct answer is C. A) 0 B) 1 C) −1 D) undefined	14. C
15. Since x^4 is a factor of x^6, the LCM of $4x^4$ and $6x^6$ is $12x^6$. A) $2x^4$ B) $12x^6$ C) $12x^{12}$ D) $24x^{24}$	15. B
16. $\pi(\pi^2+\pi) + \pi(\pi^2-\pi) = \pi^3 + \pi^2 + \pi^3 - \pi^2 = 2\pi^3.$ A) 0 B) π^3 C) $2\pi^3$ D) $2\pi^3+2\pi^2$	16. C
17. Divide both sides of the equation $3ax^2+3bx+3c = 0$ by 3 to get the equivalent equation $ax^2+bx+c = 0$ with the same roots. A) 2 and 3 B) 6 and 9 C) 18 and 27 D) −2 and −3	17. B
18. $p \div 0.5p = p \div (p/2) = p \times (2/p) = 2 = 200\%.$ A) $(1/2)\%$ B) 20% C) 50% D) 200%	18. D
19. $(\pm5,0)$, $(0,\pm5)$, $(\pm3,4)$, $(\pm3,-4)$, $(\pm4,3)$, and $(\pm4,-3)$ all satisfy $x^2+y^2 = 25$. A) twelve B) eight C) six D) four	19. A
20. $10^3 \times (1.76x)^3 = 7883$, so $(1.76x)^3 = 7.883$. A) 788.3 B) 78.83 C) 7.883 D) 0.7883	20. C
21. If $n = 3$, then n, $n+2$, and $n+4 = 3, 5,$ and 7. If $n > 3$, then n, or $n+2$, or $n+4$ is divisible by 3. A) none B) one C) two D) three	21. B

Go on to the next page ▥➡ **A**

22. Since $(1/3 + 1/x) \div 2 = 1/4$, we can solve to get $x = 6$. A) 5 B) 6 C) $\frac{1}{5}$ D) $\frac{1}{6}$	22. B
23. There are 10 different letters in the phrase, so each of the 10 digits is used once. The sum is $0+1+2+3+4+5+6+7+8+9 = 45$. A) 9 B) 10 C) 45 D) 55	23. C
24. Try $x = 100$ or 121 or 144; A is correct. A) $\sqrt{x}$ and $\sqrt{x}+1$ B) $\sqrt{x}+1$ and $\sqrt{x}+2$ C) $\sqrt{x}+2$ and $\sqrt{x}+3$ D) $\sqrt{x}+3$ and $\sqrt{x}+4$	24. A
25. $1-\frac{1}{2} + \frac{1}{2}-\frac{1}{3} + \frac{1}{3}-\frac{1}{4} + \ldots + \frac{1}{2001}-\frac{1}{2002} = 1-\frac{1}{2002} = \frac{2001}{2002}$. A) $\frac{1}{2002}$ B) $\frac{1999}{2002}$ C) $\frac{2001}{2002}$ D) 1	25. C
26. The sum of the roots is $(-1+2)+(-3+4)+ \ldots +(-99+100) = 50$. A) 100 B) 50 C) –50 D) –100	26. B
27. If $|x| = -y$, then $y < 0$; so $|y| = -y$. (Try $y = -2$, $x = 2,-2$.) A) x B) $-x$ C) y D) $-y$	27. D
28. $a^2-b^2 = (a+b)(a-b) = $ (even)(even) or (odd)(odd), so a^2-b^2 must be either a multiple of 4 *OR* odd, and 2002 is neither. A) 2002 B) 2003 C) 2004 D) 2005	28. A
29. To run two 60 km laps at 12 km/hr takes 10 hrs. 1st lap at 15 km/hr takes 4 hrs. 2nd lap takes $10-4 = 6$ hrs, so 2nd lap rate is 10 km/hr. That's 2 km/hr slower $= 16\frac{2}{3}\%$ slower than 12 km/hr. A) $\frac{50}{3}$ B) 20 C) 25 D) $\frac{250}{3}$	29. A
30. You can use just the last 2 digits of each year. Look for a number you can write as a product of digits in the greatest # of ways: $6 = 1\times6 = 2\times3 = 3\times2 = 6\times1$ (1916, 1923, 1932, 1961). Similarly, 8, 12, 24 can also be written as digit-products in 4 different ways. A) 2 B) 3 C) 4 D) 6	30. C

The end of the contest **A**

Information & Solutions

Spring, 2003

Contest Information

- **Solutions** Turn the page for detailed contest solutions (written in the question boxes) and letter answers (written in the *Answers* column to the right of each question).

- **Scores** Please remember that *this is a contest, not a test*—and there is no "passing" or "failing" score. Few students score as high as 30 points (75% correct). Students with half that, 15 points, *deserve commendation!*

- **Answers & Rating Scale** Turn to page 149 for the letter answers to each question and the rating scale for this contest.

1. If $x = 10$, then $2x^3 + 0x^2 + 0x + 3 = 2000 + 0 + 0 + 3 = 2003$. A) 23 B) 203 C) 230 D) 2003	1. D
2. Since $x^2+3x-4 = (x+4)(x-1)$, the factors are $x+4$, $x-1$, and 1. A) $x+4$ B) $x-1$ C) $x-4$ D) 1	2. C
3. Since $(n)(2003) = 2003+2003+2003+2003+2003 = 5\times2003$, $n = 5$. A) 5 B) 2001 C) 2002 D) 2003	3. A
4. $\frac{2}{x} = -1$ if $x = -2$, but $\frac{2}{x}$ is never integral if $x < -2$. A) -2 B) 2 C) -1 D) 1	4. A
5. My unfolded hat's area is s^2. Since its perimeter is $4s$, we get $\frac{s^2}{4s} = \frac{s}{4} = 4$. Solving, we get $s = 16$. A) 4 B) 8 C) 16 D) 64	5. C
6. $x+1-x+1+2+x-2+x = (x-x+x+x)+(1+1+2-2) = 2x + 2$. A) $2x$ B) $2x+2$ C) 2 D) 6	6. B
7. The number of even integers between 1 and 2003 is the same as the number of odd integers between $4 = (1+3)$ and $(2003+3)$. A) 2000 B) 2002 C) 2004 D) 2006	7. D
8. If $\frac{2001}{x} + \frac{2002}{x} + \frac{2003}{x} = 1$, then $\frac{6006}{x} = 1$ and $x = 6006$. A) 6002 B) 6004 C) 6006 D) 6008	8. C
9. This is a right triangle with base $11 - 1 = 10$ and height $11 - 1 = 10$. Its area is $(10\times10)/2 = 50$. A) 50 B) 60.5 C) 100 D) 121	9. A
10. If each letter is a different positive odd integer, the least possible value of $\sqrt{s+t+o+p}$ is $\sqrt{1+3+5+7} = \sqrt{16} = 4$. A) 2 B) 4 C) 8 D) 16	10. B
11. Since $y > 0$, we know that $\sqrt{y^8} = y^4$, $\sqrt{y^4} = y^2$, and $\sqrt{y^2} = y$. The correct answer is choice C. A) y^3 B) y^6 C) y^8 D) y^{16}	11. C

Go on to the next page ⟩ **A**

12. The least possible sum is $1 + \frac{1}{1} = 2$.

    A) 1   B) 1.5   C) 2   D) 2.5

    12.
    C

13. $(x^2+y^2)^2 = (x^2+y^2)(x^2+y^2) = x^4+x^2y^2+y^2x^2+y^4 = x^4+2x^2y^2+y^4$.

    A) xy B) $2xy$ C) x^2y^2 D) $2x^2y^2$

    13.
    D

14. If $0 < x < 1$, then $x^{1000} < 1$. Since $4/\pi > 1$, $x^{1000} \neq 4/\pi$.

    A) $\frac{1}{\pi}$ B) $\frac{2}{\pi}$ C) $\frac{3}{\pi}$ D) $\frac{4}{\pi}$

    14.
    D

15. Since $(-5)^{2002} = 5^{2002}$, $5^{2003} \div (-5)^{2002} = 5^{2003} \div 5^{2002} = 5^1 = 5$.

    A) 1   B) 5   C) –1   D) –5

    15.
    B

16. The sum must be divisible by 3. Its square must be divisible by 9.

    A) 2   B) 4   C) 9   D) 16

    16.
    C

17. If $x = 0$, then $y = \pi(0)+\pi = \pi$, so $(0,-1)$ is not on the line.

    A) $(-1,0)$ B) $(0,\pi)$ C) $(0,-1)$ D) $(1,2\pi)$

    17.
    C

18. If I rounded up 1 can of corned beef for every 4 cans of soup, then the # of cans of corned beef would be 25% of the # of cans of soup. Of every 5 cans, 4 would be soup, so the # of cans of soup was 80% of the total number of cans.

    A) 20   B) 25   C) 75   D) 80

    18.
    D

19. $(x-1)^3(x+1)^2 = (x-1)[(x-1)(x+1)]^2 = (x-1)(x^2-1)^2$.

    A) $(x-1)(x^2-1)^2$ B) $(x-1)(x^2+1)^2$
    C) $(x+1)(x^2-1)^2$ D) $(x+1)(x^2+1)^2$

    19.
    A

20. Subtract $x-y-13 = 0$ from $x+y-17 = 0$ to get $2y-4 = 0$, and $y = 2$.

    A) 2   B) 13   C) 15   D) 17

    20.
    A

21. If $(a,b) = (-3,-2)$, then $(x-a)(x+b) = (x+3)(x-2) = (x-2)(x+3)$.

    A) $(-2,-3)$ B) $(2,-3)$ C) $(-3,2)$ D) $(-3,-2)$

    21.
    D

22. $\dfrac{\frac{1}{x}+\frac{1}{y}}{x+y} = \left(\frac{1}{x}+\frac{1}{y}\right) \div (x+y) = \frac{x+y}{xy} \div (x+y) = \frac{x+y}{xy} \times \frac{1}{x+y} = \frac{1}{xy}$.

    A) 1   B) $\frac{1}{xy}$ C) xy D) $x + y$

    22.
    B

Go on to the next page ▥➡ **A**

23. The possible values of (a,b) are $(2002,1)$, $(2001,2)$, $(2000,3)$, . . . , $(1003,1000)$, and $(1002,1001)$. There are 1001 possible triangles.

    A) 1001   B) 1002   C) 2002   D) 2003

23.

A

24. Rate's constant $\Rightarrow$ dist$_1$: hrs$_1$ = dist$_2$: hrs$_2$ $\Leftrightarrow$ $\frac{k}{h} = \frac{h}{x}$. Cross-multiply to find $kx = h^2$. Solve for x to see that $x = h^2/k$, choice D.

    A) $\frac{k}{h}$ B) $\frac{h}{k}$ C) $\frac{k^2}{h}$ D) $\frac{h^2}{k}$

24.

D

25. $\frac{p}{100}(x) = 1 \Leftrightarrow \frac{x}{100} = \frac{1}{p}$, so $\frac{1}{p} \times \frac{1}{100} \times x = \frac{x^2}{10\,000}$.

    A) $\frac{x}{10000}$ B) $\frac{x^2}{10000}$ C) $\frac{x}{100}$ D) $\frac{x^2}{100}$

25.

B

26. If $2003^{x^2+2x-35} = 1$, then $x^2+2x-35 = 0$, so $x = -7$ or 5.

    A) -2 B) 2   C) -35 D) 35

26.

C

27. $5^3+91 = 6^3$, & $6^3+127 = 7^3$ so $a^3+125 = c^3$ has no pos. int. sols.

    A) 0   B) 1   C) 2   D) 3

27.

A

28. Since $1/60 > 1/65 > 1/c$, $1/60$ is the length of the hypotenuse. So, $1/c^2 + 1/65^2 = 1/60^2$ and $c = 156$.

    A) $\sqrt{7825}$ B) $3900 \div \sqrt{7825}$
    C) 70   D) 156

28.

D

29. If $a + \frac{1}{a} = 6$, then $\left(a + \frac{1}{a}\right)^2 =$ $a^2 + 2 + \frac{1}{a^2} = 6^2 = 36$. Since $a^2 + \frac{1}{a^2} = 34$, it must have taken me 34 attempts to learn how to flip flapjacks.

    A) 34   B) 35   C) 36   D) 38

29.

A

30. $9^{4a} \times 49^{2b} = (3^2)^{4a} \times (7^2)^{2b} = (3^a)^8 \times (7^b)^4 = (2)^8 \times (5)^4$.

    A) $2^4 \times 5^2$ B) $2^6 \times 5^6$ C) $2^8 \times 5^4$ D) $2^4 \times 5^8$

30.

C

The end of the contest **A**

Visit our Web site at http://www.mathleague.com

Information & Solutions

Spring, 2004

Contest Information

■ **Solutions** Turn the page for detailed contest solutions (written in the question boxes) and letter answers (written in the *Answers* column to the right of each question).

■ **Scores** Please remember that *this is a contest, not a test*—and there is no "passing" or "failing" score. Few students score as high as 24 points (80% correct). Students with half that, 12 points, *deserve commendation!*

■ **Answers & Rating Scale** Turn to page 150 for the letter answers to each question and the rating scale for this contest.

1. $(2^2)(2^0)(2^0)(2^4) = (2^2)(1)(1)(2^4) = (2^2)(2^4) = 2^6$. A) 0 B) 2^6 C) 2^8 D) 2^{2004}	1. B
2. Hairy took x minutes. Beary took 1 minute longer $= x+1$. Finally, the product of these two times is $x(x+1) = x^2+x$.  A) $2x^2+1$ B) $2x+1$ C) x^2+1 D) x^2+x	2. D
3. Since $-100 - (-10) = -100 + 10$, the answer is B. A) -110 B) -100 C) -90 D) 100	3. B
4. Order of operations: $(100 \div 10) \times 10 + (10 \times 10) = (10 \times 10) + 100 = 200$. A) 101 B) 110 C) 200 D) 1100	4. C
5. $(-1)^2+(-1)^0+(-1)^0+(-1)^4 = 1+1+1+1$. A) 2 B) 4 C) 6 D) 8	5. B
6. The only positive divisors of p^2 are 1, p, and p^2. A) 1 B) 2 C) 3 D) 4	6. C
7. $(a+b)^2 = a^2+b^2+2ab$, so $(234+567)^2 = 234^2+567^2 + 2 \times 234 \times 567$. A) 0 B) $234+567$ C) 234×567 D) 468×567	7. D
8. $\dfrac{x^2+1}{x^2} = \dfrac{x^2}{x^2}+\dfrac{1}{x^2} = 1+\dfrac{1}{x^2}$. A) $1+\dfrac{1}{x^2}$ B) $1+x^2$ C) $x^2+\dfrac{1}{x^2}$ D) $\dfrac{1}{x^2}$	8. A
9. A DVD cost 1.5 times as much as a CD, so (cost of 12 DVDs):(cost of 15 CDs) $= 12(1.5x):15(1x) = 18:15 = 6:5$. A) 4:5 B) 5:4 C) 5:6 D) 6:5	9. D
10. Mary resisted dunking her doughnut for $b\%$ of a minutes. Mary resisted dunking her doughnut for $(b/100) \times a = ab/100$ minutes.  A) ab B) $\dfrac{ab}{10}$ C) $\dfrac{ab}{100}$ D) $\dfrac{ab}{1000}$	10. C
11. $\sqrt{2^2} + \sqrt{2^4} + \sqrt{2^6} = 2^1+2^2+2^3 = 2+4+8$. A) $2+4+8$ B) $2 \times 4 \times 8$ C) $2+4+6$ D) $2 \times 4 \times 6$	11. A

Go on to the next page ▐▶ **A**

12. Since $(x+3)(x-3) = x^2-9$, it follows that $a = -9$.

A) -9 B) -3 C) 3 D) 9

| 12. |
| A |

13. If $x^2 = 5$, then $(x+1)(x-1) = x^2-1 = 5-1 = 4$.

A) -24 B) 24 C) -4 D) 4

| 13. |
| D |

14. $x(x[x(x+2)+2]+2)+2 = x(x[x^2+2x+2]+2)+2 = x(x^3+2x^2+2x+2)+2 = x^4+2x^3+2x^2+2x+2$.

A) 4 B) 5 C) 6 D) 8

| 14. |
| B |

15. $\dfrac{1}{x^2} + \dfrac{1}{y^2} = \dfrac{y^2}{x^2y^2} + \dfrac{x^2}{x^2y^2} = \dfrac{y^2+x^2}{x^2y^2} = \dfrac{x^2+y^2}{x^2y^2}$.

A) 1 B) 2 C) x^2y^2 D) x^2+y^2

| 15. |
| D |

16. The area of S is x^2. The perimeter of S is $4x$. The sum of the area and the perimeter of the square is $x^2+4x = x(x+4)$.

A) $x(x+4)$ B) $(x+2)(x+2)$ C) $(x+4)^2$ D) $4x^3$

| 16. |
| A |

17. $(x-9)^2 = 1 \Leftrightarrow x = 10$ or 8. The difference $= 10 - 8 = 2$.

A) 0 B) 2 C) 9 D) 18

| 17. |
| B |

18. $(x+3)^2 = (x+3)(x+3) = x^2+6x+9$, so x^2+6x+9 is a square.

A) x^2+x+9 B) x^2+4x+9 C) x^2+6x+9 D) x^2+9x+9

| 18. |
| C |

19. The point $(100,-100)$ is 100 units right of the y-axis and 100 units below the x-axis, so it's 100 units from both axes.

A) $(100,-100)$ B) $(0,100)$ C) $(-100,0)$ D) $(0,-100)$

| 19. |
| A |

20. The integers ±1, ±2, ±3, ±4 satisfy $(x^2-1)(x^2-4)(x^2-9)(x^2-16) = 0$.

A) 0 B) 4 C) 8 D) 16

| 20. |
| C |

And the winning number..

21. The roots of $x^2+bx+c = 0$ are 4 and 5, so $(x-4)(x-5) = x^2-9x+20 = 0$. Thus, $b = -9$ and $c = 20$. The winning number is $-9+20 = 11$.

A) 9 B) 11 C) 19 D) 21

| 21. |
| B |

Go on to the next page ⟫ **A**

22. If $x = -101$, then all 101 terms in the product are negative. A) -98 B) -99 C) -100 D) -101	22. D
23. Expand $(x+1)^n$ for $n = 1,2,3,....$ The coefficient of x^1 is always n. A) 400 B) 20 C) 19 D) 1	23. B
24. If $x = 0$, then $\frac{1}{x}$ is undefined; if $x = \pm 1$, then $x - \frac{1}{x}$ is undefined. A) 1 B) 2 C) 3 D) 4	24. C
25. $x^2+4x+4 = (x+2)^2 = (y+4)^2 = y^2+8y+16$. A) y^2+16 B) $y^2+8y+16$ C) $y^2+4y+20$ D) y^2+4y+6	25. B
26. $\sqrt{b(a+1)^3} = \sqrt{b(a+1)} \times \sqrt{(a+1)^2} = \sqrt{ab+b} \times |a+1|$ is an integer. A) $\sqrt{b(a+1)^0}$ B) $\sqrt{b(a+1)^2}$ C) $\sqrt{b(a+1)^3}$ D) $\sqrt{b(a+1)^4}$	26. C
27. Line ℓ is perpendicular to line k. If the slope of ℓ is -2, then the slope of ℓ divided by the slope of k equals $-2 \div (1/2) = -4$. A) $\frac{1}{4}$ B) $-\frac{1}{4}$ C) 4 D) -4	27. D
28. To make square as large as possible, use mostly 9s. For an even product, still a square, use two 8s. Then, $9+9+9+9+9+8+8 = 61$. A) 28 B) 58 C) 61 D) 63	28. C
29. If A/P is an integer, then $s^2/(4s) = s/4$ is an integer. Thus, s must be divisible by 4. Only choice A is divisible by 4. A) 456 B) 567 C) 678 D) 789	29. A
30. In order, the terms of the sequence are $k, 1/k, k, 1/k, \ldots, k, 1/k$. The sum of all $2n$ terms is $(n \times k) + (n \times 1/k) = nk + (n/k) = (nk^2+n)/k$. A) $\frac{nk^2+n}{k}$ B) $\frac{nk^2+n}{2k}$ C) $\frac{k^2+1}{kn}$ D) $\frac{n+k}{k^2}$	30. A

The end of the contest ✍ **A**

Information & Solutions

Spring, 2005

Contest Information

- **Solutions** Turn the page for detailed contest solutions (written in the question boxes) and letter answers (written in the *Answers* column to the right of each question).

- **Scores** Please remember that *this is a contest, not a test*—and there is no "passing" or "failing" score. Few students score as high as 24 points (80% correct). Students with half that, 12 points, *deserve commendation!*

- **Answers & Rating Scale** Turn to page 151 for the letter answers to each question and the rating scale for this contest.

1. $1^{2005} + 1^{2005} = 1 + 1 = 2 = 2^1$.

   A) 1^{4010} B) 2^1 C) 2^{2005} D) 2^{4010}

   1.

   B

2. n piles of 12 coconuts each = $(12n)$ coconuts = $(3 \times 4n)$ coconuts = $4n$ piles of 3 coconuts each.

   A) $n+3$ B) $n+4$ C) $3n$ D) $4n$

   2.

   D

3. $x^{400} \div x^{100} = x^{(400 - 100)} = x^{300}$.

   A) x^{500} B) x^{300} C) x^4 D) 4

   3.

   B

4. $(-1)^1+(-1)^2+...+(-1)^{99} = (-1)+(1)+...+(-1) = 0+...+(-1) = -1$.

   A) 1   B) 0   C) –1   D) –99

   4.

   C

5. Since $x^2-y^2 = (x+y)(x-y) = 10(x-y) = 10$, we see that $x-y = 1$.

   A) 1   B) –1   C) 10   D) –10

   5.

   A

6. Since $(2x)(5¢) + (x)(10¢) = 60¢$, add to get $20x¢ = 60¢$, so $x = 3$.

   A) 6   B) 4   C) 3   D) 2

   6.

   C

7. Since 8 is divisible by both 2 and 4, the l.c.m. of all three is 8.

   A) 2   B) 8   C) 16   D) 64

   7.

   B

8. $2 = \sqrt{4} = \sqrt{8/2} = \sqrt{8} \div \sqrt{2}$.

   A) 4   B) $\sqrt{6}$ C) $\sqrt{4}$ D) $\sqrt{2}$

   8.

   D

9. If $h = $ # of light helmets, then $2h = $ # of dark helmets. There are 6 more dark helmets than light ones, so $2h-h = 6$, or $h = 6$. The number of light helmets is 6.

   A) 2   B) 3   C) 6   D) 12

   9.

   C

10. Any 2 lines of the form $2x+y = k$, with unequal k's, are parallel.

    A) $2x+y = 3$ B) $2x+4y = 6$ C) $2x-y = 3$ D) $x+2y = -3$

    10.

    A

11. The average is x, so the integers are $x-2$, $x-1$, x, $x+1$, and $x+2$.

    A) $x-2$ B) $x-3$ C) $x-4$ D) $x-5$

    11.

    A

Go on to the next page ⏵ **A**

12. The average is x, so the integers are $x-4$, $x-2$, x, $x+2$, and $x+4$. A) $x-2$ B) $x-3$ C) $x-4$ D) $x-5$	12. C
13. 2^{2004} is a factor of 2^{2005}, so 2^{2004} is the g.c.f. A) 1 B) 2 C) 2^{2004} D) 2^{2005}	13. C
14. A horizontal line is parallel to the x-axis. I was the 7th caller to know that the slope of any such line is 0. A) 0 B) 1 C) –1 D) nonexistent	14. A
15. $a = 100\%$ of $a = 10 \times 10\%$ of $a = 10b$. A) $0.1b$ B) b C) $9b$ D) $10b$	15. D
16. When $n = 6$, $n^n = 6^6 = \left(6^{6/2}\right)^2 = (6^3)^2$, which is the square of 6^3. A) 3 B) 5 C) 6 D) 7	16. C
17. If $k = 4$, then $x^2+4x+4 = (x+2)(x+2) = 0$ and $x = -2$ or -2. A) 1 B) 2 C) 3 D) 4	17. D
18. Jesse has worn the same hat for d years. If he wears it for 12 more years, he will have worn this hat for d^2 years. So, $d+12 = d^2$, or $(d+3)(d-4) = 0$. Since $d > 0$, $d = 4$. A) 4 B) 6 C) 8 D) 12	18. A
19. $|x| + |-x| = |x| + |x| = 2|x|$. A) 0 B) $|x|$ C) $|-x|$ D) $2|x|$	19. D
20. Sketch circle C. Of the choices, only choice A, (0,5), is on circle C. A) (0,5) B) (−5,−5) C) (−10,0) D) (5,5)	20. A
21. The 4 positive factors of ab are 1, a, b, and ab. A) 4 B) 3 C) 2 D) 1	21. A
22. Since $(-x)^{100} = (-1)^{100}(x^{100}) = 1 \times x^{100}$, choice B is correct. A) 100 B) 1 C) –1 D) –100	22. B

Go on to the next page ⫸ **A**

131

23. $\sqrt{16^{16}} = \sqrt{(16^8)^2} = 16^8$.

    A) 16^8 B) 16^4 C) 4^8 D) 4^4

23.

A

---

24. $A = \pi r^2 = 3600\pi$, so $r^2 = 3600$, or $r = 60$. $C = 2\pi r$, so $C = 120\pi$.

    A) 60   B) 60π C) 120   D) 120π

24.

D

---

25. If $(n^2-1)(n^2-2)(n^2-3) = 0$, then $n^2-1 = 0$, or $n^2-2 = 0$, or $n^2-3 = 0$. Therefore, $n^2 = 1$, or $n^2 = 2$, or $n^2 = 3$. The only integers which satisfy any of these equations are 1 and –1. The number of times I moved by mail is 2.

    A) 1   B) 2   C) 3   D) 6

25.

B

---

26. $\dfrac{y}{xy} + \dfrac{x}{xy} + \dfrac{1}{xy} = \dfrac{x+y+1}{xy}$.

    A) 2   B) 3   C) $x+y+1$ D) $x+y$

26.

C

---

27. If $x^2 + y^2 = (x + y)^2$, then $x^2 + y^2 = x^2 + 2xy + y^2$. Thus, $2xy = 0$, so $xy = 0$.

    A) 0   B) 1   C) 4   D) 16

27.

A

---

28. $(x^2+2x+1)+(x^2+4x+4)+(x^2+6x+9)-[(x^2+1)+(x^2+4)+(x^2+9)] = 12x$.

    A) 0   B) $6x$ C) $9x$ D) $12x$

28.

D

---

29. Using $x > 0$, $\dfrac{x}{x+1} < \dfrac{2004}{2005} \Leftrightarrow x < 2004$. The largest integral solution is $x = 2003$. The sum of the digits of 2003 is 5, so I swam with 5 fish.

    A) 4   B) 5   C) 6   D) 7

29.

B

---

30. There are 5 ways to factor –16 into 2 integral factors (-16×1, -8×2, -4×4, -2×8, and -1×16). Their sum is the value of b.

    A) 3   B) 4   C) 5   D) 6

30.

C

The end of the contest ✍ **A**

Information & Solutions

Spring, 2006

Contest Information

- **Solutions** Turn the page for detailed contest solutions (written in the question boxes) and letter answers (written in the *Answers* column to the right of each question).

- **Scores** Please remember that *this is a contest, not a test*—and there is no "passing" or "failing" score. Few students score as high as 24 points (80% correct). Students with half that, 12 points, *deserve commendation!*

- **Answers & Rating Scale** Turn to page 152 for the letter answers to each question and the rating scale for this contest.

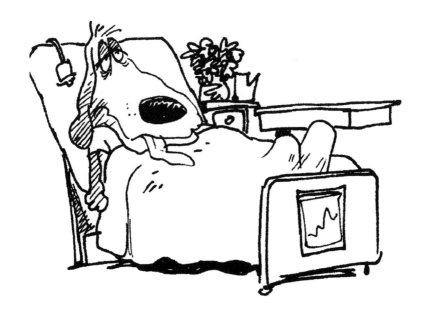

1. $(2+0+0+6)^{(2\times0\times0\times6)} = 8^0 = 1.$

   A) 1   B) 8   C) 0   D) 8^8

   1.
   A

---

2. Given $= (-2)(1)(-2)(2)(-2)(3)(-2)(4)(-2)(5) = (1)(2)(3)(4)(5)(-32).$

   A) 2   B) -2 C) 32   D) -32

   2.
   D

---

3. Since $(x+1)+(2x+2) = 3x+3 = 3(x+1),$
   $(x+1)+(2x+2)$ scoops cost $3\times\$3 = \$9.$

   A) \$18   B) \$15
   C) \$12   D) \$9

   3.
   D

---

4. $8 = \dfrac{x^2-4}{x+2} = \dfrac{(x+2)(x-2)}{x+2} = x-2.$

   A) 10 B) 8 C) 6 D) 4

   4.
   B

---

5. $(10x)^{100} = 10^{100}x^{100} = (10x^{100})(10^{99}).$

   A) 1   B) 10   C) 10^{99} D) 10^{100}

   5.
   C

---

6. If $x = 0.5$, then $x^2-x = (0.5)^2-0.5 = 0.25-0.5 = -0.25 < 0.$

   A) 2   B) 1   C) 0.5   D) -0.5

   6.
   C

---

7. Clearing fractions, $\dfrac{x}{3} < 3 \Leftrightarrow x < 9.$ Since $x > 0, x = 1, 2, \ldots, 8.$

   A) 9   B) 8   C) 6   D) 3

   7.
   B

---

8. Since area $= lw, l:w = 48:1$ or $24:2,$ or $16:3,$ or $12:4,$ or $8:6.$
   Choice B is not included among these possibilities.

   A) $3:1$ B) $6:1$ C) $12:1$ D) $48:1$

   8.
   B

---

9. The ratio of the number of teams that wear red
   jerseys to the number that wear blue is 7:13. Of
   20 teams, 7 wear red jerseys, so the percent
   that wear red jerseys is $7/20 = 35/100 = 35\%.$

   A) 70%   B) 49%   C) 35%   D) 20%

   9.
   C

---

10. The first multiple of x^2 that's divisible by $2x$ is $2x^2.$

    A) $2x$ B) $2x^2$ C) $2x^3$ D) $2x^4$

    10.
    B

---

11. $x^{18}+2x^{17}+x^{16} = x^{16}(x^2+2x+1) = x^{16}(x+1)^2.$

    A) x^4 B) x^8 C) x^{12} D) x^{16}

    11.
    D

Go on to the next page ⫸ **A**

12.	I was in the hospital for $\|2x\|+\|-x\|$ days $= 2\|x\|+\|x\|$ days $= 3\|x\|$ days.  A) $3x$ B) x C) $\|x\|$ D) $3\|x\|$	12. D
13.	Rewrite each choice as shown below. Choice A is largest if $x > 1$. A) x^{50} B) x^{20} C) $x^{10}x^5 = x^{15}$ D) $x^2x^{25} = x^{27}$	13. A
14.	$x = \pm\sqrt{2006}$. The product is $-\sqrt{2006} \times \sqrt{2006} = -2006$. A) 2006 B) 5002 C) $2\sqrt{2006}$ D) -2006	14. D
15.	Each side has length $(x+1)^2$. Perimeter $= 4s = 4(x+1)^2$. A) $4(x+1)^2$ B) $(x+1)^2$ C) $4(x+1)$ D) $(4x+1)$	15. A
16.	$\dfrac{w^2w^4w^6\times\ldots\times w^{48}w^{50}}{w^1w^3w^5\times\ldots\times w^{47}w^{49}} = \dfrac{w^2}{w^1}\times\dfrac{w^4}{w^3}\times\ldots\times\dfrac{w^{50}}{w^{49}} = w^{25}$. A) w^{24} B) w^{25} C) w^{49} D) w^{50}	16. B
17.	Any positive integer that's both a perfect square and a perfect cube is of the form n^6, where n is an integer. The only such integers less than 100 are $1^6 = 1$ and $2^6 = 64$.  A) 1 B) 2 C) 3 D) 64	17. B
18.	Parallel lines have equal slopes. The number 2 cannot be written as a product of three identical integers. A) $-1 \times -1 \times -1$ B) $0 \times 0 \times 0$ C) $1 \times 1 \times 1$ D) 2	18. D
19.	If $y = 2x+5$, then $3y = 6x+15$; so $a = 6$, $b = 15$, and $a+b = 21$. A) 7 B) 13 C) 21 D) 30	19. C
20.	My age in years is a two-digit number. Reversing the digits of my age results in my age 18 years ago. So, $10u+t = 10t+u-18$. Thus, $9t-9u = 18$ or $t-u = 2$. A) 1 B) 2 C) 3 D) 4	20. B
21.	$\sqrt{M \times A \times T \times M \times A \times T} = M \times A \times T$, so H must be $M \times A \times T$. A) $M \times A \times T$ B) $\sqrt{M \times A \times T}$ C) $M^2 \times A^2 \times T^2$ D) 1	21. A

Go on to the next page ⫸ **A**

22. We're told that $10d+5n = 25(n-d)$, so $10d+5n = 25n-25d$, from which $35d = 20n$. Dividing by $35n$, $d{:}n = 20{:}35 = 4{:}7$.

    A) 4:7   B) 7:4   C) 1:2   D) 2:1

    22. A

23. From the 99 integers $\{1, \ldots , 99\}$, choose n different integers. Since $100 = 1\times2\times5\times10$, the greatest possible value of n is 4.

    A) 2   B) 3   C) 4   D) 5

    23. C

24. Undefined $\Leftrightarrow x+2006 = 0$ or $x+\dfrac{2005}{x+2006} = 0$. In the latter case, $x^2+2006x+2005 = (x+2005)(x+1) = 0$; so $x = -2006, -2005, -1$.

    A) 1   B) 2   C) 3   D) 4

    24. C

25. The smallest such number is the square root of 4^{144}, which is 4^{72}.

    A) 4^{12} B) 4^{72} C) 4^{144} D) 4^{288}

    25. B

26. $x-y + \dfrac{1}{x+y} = \dfrac{(x-y)(x+y)+1}{x+y} = \dfrac{x^2-y^2+1}{x+y}$, so $\star = -y^2$.

    A) $-y^2$ B) xy C) y^2 D) $-xy$

    26. A

27. The roots of $x^2 = a^2$ are roots of $(x^2)^2 = (a^2)^2 \Leftrightarrow x^4-a^4 = 0$.

    A) $x-a = 0$ B) $x+a = 0$ C) $x^2+a^2 = 0$ D) $x^4-a^4 = 0$

    27. D

28. Try $(-2,1)$ in QII. Change both signs to get $(2,-1)$ in QIV.

    A) I   B) II   C) III   D) IV

    28. D

29. The whole-number factors of 64 are $1, 2^1, 2^2, 2^3, 2^4, 2^5, 2^6$. The product of these is $1\times2^1\times2^2\times2^3\times2^4\times2^5\times2^6 = 2^{1+2+3+4+5+6} = 2^{21}$.

    A) 2^{36} B) 2^{21} C) 2^{12} D) 2^{11}

    29. B

30. Given $\Leftrightarrow 1 < |x+1| \Leftrightarrow x+1 < -1$ or $x+1 > 1 \Leftrightarrow x < -2$ or $x > 0$.

    A) $x < -2$ B) $x > -1$ C) $x < 0$ D) $x < 1$

    30. A

The end of the contest **A**

Answer Keys & Difficulty Ratings

2001-2002 through 2005-2006

ANSWERS, 2001-02 7th Grade Contest

1. C	9. C	17. A	25. B	33. C
2. D	10. B	18. B	26. A	34. B
3. C	11. D	19. D	27. D	35. A
4. B	12. B	20. A	28. C	36. B
5. D	13. A	21. B	29. B	37. B
6. A	14. B	22. D	30. B	38. A
7. D	15. D	23. C	31. C	39. C
8. A	16. C	24. C	32. D	40. D

RATE YOURSELF!!!
for the 2001-02 7th GRADE CONTEST

Score	Rating
37-40	Another Einstein
34-36	Mathematical Wizard
31-33	School Champion
29-30	Grade Level Champion
26-28	Best In The Class
22-25	Excellent Student
18-21	Good Student
14-17	Average Student
0-13	Better Luck Next Time

ANSWERS, 2002-03 7th Grade Contest

1. A	9. D	17. D	25. C	33. C
2. B	10. A	18. B	26. A	34. A
3. A	11. D	19. B	27. C	35. B
4. B	12. D	20. C	28. B	36. B
5. C	13. B	21. A	29. D	37. D
6. C	14. B	22. D	30. B	38. C
7. C	15. C	23. A	31. C	39. B
8. B	16. A	24. D	32. A	40. C

RATE YOURSELF!!!
for the 2002-03 7th GRADE CONTEST

Score	Rating
38-40	Another Einstein
35-37	Mathematical Wizard
33-34	School Champion
30-32	Grade Level Champion
27-29	Best In The Class
24-26	Excellent Student
19-23	Good Student
15-18	Average Student
0-14	Better Luck Next Time

ANSWERS, 2003-04 7th Grade Contest

1. A	9. B	17. B	25. D	33. A
2. D	10. D	18. D	26. B	34. B
3. D	11. A	19. C	27. C	35. D
4. C	12. B	20. B	28. A	36. C
5. D	13. B	21. A	29. B	37. C
6. C	14. A	22. C	30. A	38. A
7. C	15. A	23. D	31. C	39. D
8. B	16. D	24. C	32. B	40. A

RATE YOURSELF!!!
for the 2003-04 7th GRADE CONTEST

Score	Rating
39-40	Another Einstein
36-38	Mathematical Wizard
33-35	School Champion
30-32	Grade Level Champion
27-29	Best In The Class
24-26	Excellent Student
21-23	Good Student
17-20	Average Student
0-16	Better Luck Next Time

ANSWERS, 2004-05 7th Grade Contest

1. C	9. B	17. A	25. B	33. A
2. D	10. A	18. D	26. A	34. D
3. D	11. A	19. D	27. A	35. B
4. C	12. B	20. D	28. C	36. A
5. B	13. A	21. C	29. A	37. B
6. C	14. D	22. C	30. D	38. D
7. C	15. C	23. D	31. B	39. D
8. B	16. C	24. B	32. C	40. C

RATE YOURSELF!!!
for the 2004-05 7th GRADE CONTEST

Score	Rating
38-40	Another Einstein
35-37	Mathematical Wizard
33-34	School Champion
29-32	Grade Level Champion
26-28	Best In The Class
22-25	Excellent Student
19-21	Good Student
15-18	Average Student
0-14	Better Luck Next Time

ANSWERS, 2005-06 7th Grade Contest

1. B	9. B	17. C	25. B	33. B
2. C	10. B	18. D	26. A	34. B
3. C	11. D	19. C	27. C	35. D
4. B	12. C	20. B	28. B	36. D
5. D	13. A	21. A	29. D	37. B
6. D	14. D	22. D	30. B	38. A
7. A	15. C	23. C	31. C	39. B
8. A	16. A	24. A	32. D	40. C

RATE YOURSELF!!!
for the 2005-06 7th GRADE CONTEST

Score	Rating
37-40	Another Einstein
34-36	Mathematical Wizard
31-33	School Champion
28-30	Grade Level Champion
25-27	Best In The Class
21-24	Excellent Student
18-20	Good Student
15-17	Average Student
0-14	Better Luck Next Time

ANSWERS, 2001-02 8th Grade Contest

1. C	9. D	17. B	25. D	33. B
2. D	10. D	18. A	26. C	34. A
3. B	11. B	19. D	27. B	35. D
4. C	12. A	20. A	28. D	36. B
5. A	13. B	21. C	29. B	37. B
6. B	14. A	22. A	30. C	38. A
7. C	15. D	23. B	31. D	39. C
8. C	16. C	24. C	32. C	40. B

RATE YOURSELF!!!
for the 2001-02 8th GRADE CONTEST

Score	Rating
37-40	Another Einstein
34-36	Mathematical Wizard
31-33	School Champion
28-30	Grade Level Champion
25-27	Best In The Class
22-24	Excellent Student
19-21	Good Student
16-18	Average Student
0-15	Better Luck Next Time

ANSWERS, 2002-03 8th Grade Contest

1. D	9. A	17. C	25. A	33. A
2. D	10. B	18. D	26. A	34. A
3. A	11. B	19. B	27. C	35. A
4. B	12. A	20. B	28. A	36. A
5. C	13. C	21. C	29. B	37. C
6. C	14. A	22. D	30. C	38. D
7. D	15. C	23. D	31. B	39. B
8. C	16. A	24. B	32. D	40. D

RATE YOURSELF!!!
for the 2002-03 8th GRADE CONTEST

Score	Rating
37-40	Another Einstein
33-36	Mathematical Wizard
31-32	School Champion
28-30	Grade Level Champion
25-27	Best In The Class
22-24	Excellent Student
19-21	Good Student
15-18	Average Student
0-14	Better Luck Next Time

ANSWERS, 2003-04 8th Grade Contest

1. B	9. B	17. C	25. B	33. C
2. A	10. D	18. B	26. C	34. D
3. B	11. B	19. C	27. C	35. D
4. C	12. A	20. D	28. D	36. A
5. A	13. D	21. A	29. B	37. C
6. C	14. D	22. A	30. A	38. B
7. B	15. A	23. D	31. C	39. D
8. C	16. B	24. D	32. B	40. C

RATE YOURSELF!!!
for the 2003-04 8th GRADE CONTEST

Score	Rating
38-40	Another Einstein
35-37	Mathematical Wizard
33-34	School Champion
30-32	Grade Level Champion
27-29	Best In The Class
24-26	Excellent Student
20-23	Good Student
16-19	Average Student
0-15	Better Luck Next Time

ANSWERS, 2004-05 8th Grade Contest

1. D	9. A	17. A	25. B	33. C
2. A	10. C	18. A	26. D	34. D
3. C	11. A	19. D	27. B	35. C
4. D	12. D	20. C	28. C	36. A
5. B	13. B	21. A	29. A	37. C
6. B	14. D	22. C	30. B	38. C
7. C	15. C	23. B	31. D	39. B
8. A	16. B	24. D	32. A	40. D

RATE YOURSELF!!!
for the 2004-05 8th GRADE CONTEST

Score	Rating
37-40	Another Einstein
33-36	Mathematical Wizard
30-32	School Champion
26-29	Grade Level Champion
23-25	Best In The Class
20-22	Excellent Student
17-19	Good Student
14-16	Average Student
0-13	Better Luck Next Time

ANSWERS, 2005-06 8th Grade Contest

1. C	9. A	17. A	25. A	33. C
2. A	10. D	18. B	26. C	34. B
3. D	11. D	19. A	27. D	35. C
4. B	12. D	20. C	28. C	36. C
5. D	13. A	21. D	29. A	37. D
6. C	14. A	22. C	30. D	38. A
7. B	15. D	23. A	31. B	39. C
8. C	16. B	24. C	32. A	40. B

RATE YOURSELF!!!
for the 2005-06 8th GRADE CONTEST

Score	Rating
37-40	Another Einstein
34-36	Mathematical Wizard
32-33	School Champion
29-31	Grade Level Champion
27-28	Best In The Class
24-26	Excellent Student
20-23	Good Student
15-19	Average Student
0-14	Better Luck Next Time

ANSWERS, 2001-02 Algebra Course 1 Contest

1. A	7. C	13. D	19. A	25. C
2. C	8. B	14. C	20. C	26. B
3. B	9. D	15. B	21. B	27. D
4. B	10. D	16. C	22. B	28. A
5. D	11. C	17. B	23. C	29. A
6. C	12. C	18. D	24. A	30. C

RATE YOURSELF!!!
for the 2001-02 ALGEBRA COURSE 1 CONTEST

Score	Rating
27-30	Another Einstein
23-26	Mathematical Wizard
20-22	School Champion
18-19	Grade Level Champion
16-17	Best In The Class
13-15	Excellent Student
11-12	Good Student
9-10	Average Student
0-8	Better Luck Next Time

ANSWERS, 2002-03 Algebra Course 1 Contest

1. D	7. D	13. D	19. A	25. B
2. C	8. C	14. D	20. A	26. C
3. A	9. A	15. B	21. D	27. A
4. A	10. B	16. C	22. B	28. D
5. C	11. C	17. C	23. A	29. A
6. B	12. C	18. D	24. D	30. C

RATE YOURSELF!!!
for the 2002-03 ALGEBRA COURSE 1 CONTEST

Score	Rating
28-30	Another Einstein
25-27	Mathematical Wizard
22-24	School Champion
19-21	Grade Level Champion
17-18	Best In The Class
15-16	Excellent Student
13-14	Good Student
11-12	Average Student
0-10	Better Luck Next Time

ANSWERS, 2003-04 Algebra Course 1 Contest

1. B	7. D	13. D	19. A	25. B
2. D	8. A	14. B	20. C	26. C
3. B	9. D	15. D	21. B	27. D
4. C	10. C	16. A	22. D	28. C
5. B	11. A	17. B	23. B	29. A
6. C	12. A	18. C	24. C	30. A

RATE YOURSELF!!!
for the 2003-04 ALGEBRA COURSE 1 CONTEST

Score	Rating
28-30	Another Einstein
25-27	Mathematical Wizard
22-24	School Champion
20-21	Grade Level Champion
18-19	Best In The Class
15-17	Excellent Student
13-14	Good Student
10-12	Average Student
0-9	Better Luck Next Time

ANSWERS, 2004-05 Algebra Course 1 Contest

1. B	7. B	13. C	19. D	25. B
2. D	8. D	14. A	20. A	26. C
3. B	9. C	15. D	21. A	27. A
4. C	10. A	16. C	22. B	28. D
5. A	11. A	17. D	23. A	29. B
6. C	12. C	18. A	24. D	30. C

RATE YOURSELF!!!
for the 2004-05 ALGEBRA COURSE 1 CONTEST

Score	Rating
28-30	Another Einstein
25-27	Mathematical Wizard
22-24	School Champion
19-21	Grade Level Champion
17-18	Best In The Class
15-16	Excellent Student
13-14	Good Student
11-12	Average Student
0-10	Better Luck Next Time

ANSWERS, 2005-06 Algebra Course 1 Contest

1. A	7. B	13. A	19. C	25. B
2. D	8. B	14. D	20. B	26. A
3. D	9. C	15. A	21. A	27. D
4. B	10. B	16. B	22. A	28. D
5. C	11. D	17. B	23. C	29. B
6. C	12. D	18. D	24. C	30. A

RATE YOURSELF!!!
for the 2005-06 ALGEBRA COURSE 1 CONTEST

Score	Rating
27-30	Another Einstein
24-26	Mathematical Wizard
20-23	School Champion
18-19	Grade Level Champion
16-17	Best In The Class
14-15	Excellent Student
11-13	Good Student
9-10	Average Student
0-8	Better Luck Next Time

Math League Contest Books
4th Grade Through High School Levels

Written by Steven R. Conrad and Daniel Flegler, recipients of President Reagan's 1985 Presidential Awards for Excellence in Mathematics Teaching, each book provides schools and students with:

- *Easy-to-use format designed for a 30-minute period*
- *Problems ranging from straightforward to challenging*

Use the form below (or a copy) to order your books

Name: _____

Address: _____

City: _____ State: _____ Zip: _____

                       (or Province)   (or Postal Code)

Available Titles	# of Copies	Cost
Math Contests—Grades 4, 5, 6	($12.95 each, $15.95 Canadian)	
Volume 1: 1979-80 through 1985-86	_____	_____
Volume 2: 1986-87 through 1990-91	_____	_____
Volume 3: 1991-92 through 1995-96	_____	_____
Volume 4: 1996-97 through 2000-01	_____	_____
Volume 5: 2001-02 through 2005-06	_____	_____
Math Contests—Grades 7 & 8 ‡	‡(Vols. 3,4,5 include Alg. Course I)	
Volume 1: 1977-78 through 1981-82	_____	_____
Volume 2: 1982-83 through 1990-91	_____	_____
Volume 3: 1991-92 through 1995-96	_____	_____
Volume 4: 1996-97 through 2000-01	_____	_____
Volume 5: 2001-02 through 2005-06	_____	_____
Math Contests—High School		
Volume 1: 1977-78 through 1981-82	_____	_____
Volume 2: 1982-83 through 1990-91	_____	_____
Volume 3: 1991-92 through 1995-96	_____	_____
Volume 4: 1996-97 through 2000-01	_____	_____
Volume 5: 2001-02 through 2005-06	_____	_____
Shipping and Handling	$3 ($5 Canadian)	

Please allow 4-6 weeks for delivery   Total: $_____

☐ Check or Purchase Order Enclosed; *or*

☐ Visa / MasterCard/Discover # _____

☐ Exp. Date _____ Signature _____

Mail your order with payment to:
Math League Press. PO Box 17, Tenafly, New Jersey USA 07670-0017
or order on the Web at www.mathleague.com

Phone: (201) 568-6328 • Fax: (201) 816-0125